Informal Learning in Organizations

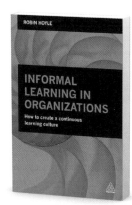

Informal Learning in Organizations

How to create
a continuous
learning culture

Robin Hoyle

KoganPage

LONDON PHILADELPHIA NEW DELHI

First published in Great Britain and the United States in 2015 by Kogan Page Limited

Apart from any fair dealing for the purposes of research or private study, or criticism or review, as permitted under the Copyright, Designs and Patents Act 1988, this publication may only be reproduced, stored or transmitted, in any form or by any means, with the prior permission in writing of the publishers, or in the case of reprographic reproduction in accordance with the terms and licences issued by the CLA. Enquiries concerning reproduction outside these terms should be sent to the publishers at the undermentioned addresses:

2nd Floor, 45 Gee Street	1518 Walnut Street,	4737/23 Ansari Road
London EC1V 3RS	Suite 1100	Daryaganj
United Kingdom	Philadelphia PA 19102	New Delhi 110002
www.koganpage.com	USA	India

© Robin Hoyle, 2015

The right of Robin Hoyle to be identified as the author of this work has been asserted by him in accordance with the Copyright, Designs and Patents Act 1988.

ISBN   978 0 7494 7459 1
E-ISBN 978 0 7494 7460 7

British Library Cataloguing-in-Publication Data

A CIP record for this book is available from the British Library.

Library of Congress Cataloging-in-Publication Data

Hoyle, Robin.
    Informal learning in organizations: how to create a continuous learning culture/Robin Hoyle. — 1st Edition.
        pages cm
    ISBN 978-0-7494-7459-1 (paperback) — ISBN 978-0-7494-7460-7 (E-ISBN)
1. Organizational change. 2. Employees—Training of. 3. Non-formal education. I. Title.
    HD58.8.H697 2015
    658.3'124—dc23
                                                2015021106

Typeset by SPi Global
Print production managed by Jellyfish
Printed and bound by CPI Group (UK) Ltd, Croydon, CR0 4YY

For my parents, Betty and Derek Hoyle, from whom I learned a lot, and for Jan Holden, from whom I learn still

Contents

ACKNOWLEDGEMENTS

As with any book of this kind, I have relied on significant help and assistance in marshalling my thoughts and determining the direction of the research I have undertaken.

I am grateful for the support, feedback and insights from editors Lucy Carter and Katy Hamilton at Kogan Page.

I am indebted to the interviewees who helped me with insights into their own experiences and shaped my ideas for the practical ways in which informal learning could be supported, specifically: Frank Clayton, Chris McGrath, Andy Bones, Andrea Efstathiou and Gemma Novo at NG Bailey; John Crossan at PB Coaching; Jason Pitfield, Rodney Assock, Nicola Rathbone, Sarah Booth, Kim Ewin-Hill, Tash Govier, Lee Beck, Hannah McQueen, Mike Turnbull, Jemma Green and Al Smith at LV=; Helen Barker, and Amanda Hudson at Bradford Royal Infirmary Teaching Hospitals Trust; Calum Holden Cooper for insights into the education of specialist nurses at Great Ormond Street Hospital; Tony Coates and Eleni Iatridis at Assima; Arnold Jung at SAP Norge SA; Faez Ahmed at ServiceNow; Mike Dowsey at the Computer Education Managers' Association Europe; Monika Agocs, Barry Neville and Kristin Wolfe at SABMiller PLC; Dr Louise Donnelly at Edinburgh University and Martin Couzins and Sam Burroughs at MOOCPro. I'd also like to thank my father, Derek Hoyle, who shared his post-war experiences as an apprentice joiner.

I am grateful also to Tracy Shah and her colleagues at the World of Learning Conference. A couple of the chapters in the book are extended versions of blogs originally published by Jon Kennard at TrainingZone.co.uk. For fruitful conversations I'd like to thank Ilsa Hoyle and Hamish Hoyle for stridently sharing their millennial flavoured impressions of social media.

Above all, I am forever in the debt of Jan Holden for her support, encouragement and advice. She has selflessly put aside her own work to read every draft of every chapter and has provided incredibly useful feedback while remaining unerringly positive.

Without the support and time of all these people this book wouldn't have happened. They have set me on the right track, corrected my wilder assertions and given me constant food for thought. Any errors or omissions are, of course, entirely my own.

Introduction

In 21st-century organizations, learning is not an optional extra but a process that is embedded in the everyday. We all learn. We all learn pretty much all the time, kind of. Organizations are under a peculiar pressure to somehow manage this day-to-day learning, learning that we have come to describe as informal.

The same is not true of other elements of organizational life. Take communications. Most businesses, public sector agencies and charities of any size will have an internal communications team. They will manage the release of information to ensure a common message reaches all employees. But beyond that, no one tries to manage the informal communication between colleagues. I can't really imagine what would happen if they did – water cooler gossip police, perhaps.

In that sense it seems counter-intuitive perhaps to try to manage something that is supposed to be informal. If learning happens all the time, if it is truly embedded in the work we all do every day, then organizations shouldn't really need to be involved at all. Maybe their greatest contribution to this ongoing development of skills and knowledge is to stay out of the way? The fear is that although organizations can't do much to manage informal learning, they can – often unwittingly – stop it happening altogether.

Well, yes and no. This book is about what happens when organizations take different approaches to learning. At one end of the organizational spectrum are those employers who believe – contrary to both evidence and common sense – that learning only happens in classrooms or at the end of online modules. It is prescriptive, descriptive and most definitely formal. In these organizations learning happens in training suites with PowerPoint presentations and flip charts. It happens in the world of learning management systems which launch eLearning modules during which learners complete multiple-choice quizzes and are signed off as competent as a result.

In this kind of enterprise, if informal learning happens at all, it is not really the concern of the employer or the HR team which manages the learning and development function. Informal learning – like some kind of alchemical mystery – is left to the misunderstood and 'can't be organized' box and therefore is left unorganized, or more commonly, disorganized. Those with initiative, a quality often asked for and rarely defined, manage to somehow plug any skills gaps. In practical terms though, the organization relies on a combination of courses and recruiting someone who has done the exact same job somewhere else.

The opposite of this classroom-dependent organization is one that takes a view that is gaining significant credibility in some quarters of the learning and development field. This group has been seduced by the growth of technology, particularly social media, into imagining a world where, to quote Pink Floyd, 'we don't need no education'. The double negative alone belies the requirement for some form of basic instruction at least.

With the growth of internet tools and our newly minted abilities to share information over time and distance with peers we may never know outside of their digital selves, the idea of disintermediated learning has taken hold. It mirrors a kind of libertarian view of the internet as a democratizing force that empowers and enables learning and discovery to take place. Through a new mantra, that of 70:20:10, the 10 per cent is the formal learning component, the remaining 70 per cent of one's learning activities being on the job and 20 per cent through networking and sharing with peers. Or – as it is often described by those with a product to sell – 90 per cent of the learning is informal.

The attitude of some in organizations who have heard that 90 per cent of learning happens informally – and believe that this is supported by both quantitative and qualitative evidence – is a painfully obvious one when faced with the expense of organizing courses, buying Learning Management Systems and building eLearning programmes. If all that money only delivers 10 per cent of the learning we need, let's not bother. Let's save the cash and rely on the initiative, desire and enthusiasm for the job in our employees to undertake the 90 per cent which will keep us as a competent, capable, not to say world beating organization.

What could go wrong? Well, quite a lot actually. As ill-conceived as the reliance purely on the classroom is, it is no more daft than neoliberal anti-teacher rhetoric. Certainly, one can hardly spend time with any parents of school age children without hearing at least one diatribe against teachers. It is fashionable to ridicule or complain about those who seek to impart knowledge. Trainers are often tarred with the same brush.

Jay Cross, in his 2007 book *Informal Learning: Rediscovering the natural pathways that inspire innovation and performance*, said: 'School is a time-consuming and generally ineffective way to learn; most corporate training is wasted effort.' [1]

However, the elevation of the insulting old saw 'those who *can* do, those who *can't* teach' to a workforce development strategy seems an example of the poor binary thinking I will examine in this book. You can't understand how people work on an either/or basis. The truth is we need good formal learning and effective informal learning. In fact, I would go a stage further and say that effective formal trainers encourage, harness and enable informal learning to happen.

Thankfully there are organizations that inhabit neither end of this formal/informal spectrum. They recognize that while informal learning can exist independently of formal programmes, courses and modules, the reverse of this is rarely true. For a formal programme to result in learning that actually enables people to do different things, training courses must require learners to take some tentative steps to try things out, to experience through trial and error, to reflect on lived experience and to discuss and connect with others. They have realized that informal learning enjoys a greater impact when it happens in line with, and supported by, more formal approaches with the input of leaders and trainers.

Why *this* book?

As someone who has picked up this book and read thus far, you have already proved yourself to be engaged in your own learning journey. You have chosen to learn more about how informal learning can be more effectively integrated into the work of organizations. Through the course of researching and writing this book, I have interviewed many involved in the middle ground of informal learning – those who seem to me to have successfully integrated learner-directed activity alongside more formal learning approaches. These organizations have recognized that 'informal' doesn't translate to either unmanaged or unsupported. They are actively seeking to be as efficient as possible without compromising the effectiveness of the capability journey which every organization is and should be making.

I've also looked at some of the examples that give me pause for thought and that are cautionary tales for those seeking to build their organization's capability as enablers of informal learning.

I have spoken to organizations that rely on knowledge workers, those at the cutting edge of technology and those who do relatively straightforward things but require greater efficiency, more quickly and with lower costs than ever before. I've also spoken to those working in situations where effective decision-making is literally a matter of life and death and where the cost of incompetence is incredibly high. In some of these organizations, leaving learning to chance could be criminally negligent.

Each chapter breaks down some of the ways in which informal learning happens. Each is examined from a critical perspective – seeking to identify the optimum conditions for informal learning within a myriad different workplace challenges. Each is illustrated by different stories and case studies. By situating the informal learning activity within the reality of what actually happens – rather than unsubstantiated hype and hyperbole – the intention is that you will be able to reflect upon your own practice and implement meaningful changes to how learning happens for you, your organizations and your colleagues.

The book is divided into three sections:

Section One: Making sense of informal learning at work sets out an overview of informal learning, within and outside the world of work.

Section Two: Liking ain't learning: the rise of social and the impact of technology provides a critique of the use of technology as a driver and enabler of informal learning. This section covers the opportunities that the internet and connectivity provide and the limitations of the new media to facilitate capability improvement.

Section Three: Learning as you work, working as you learn provides a series of tips and hints about integrating learning and work including some suggestions to help you assess your specific needs and take action to enhance informal learning in your organization.

The final chapter at the end of Section Three is about taking action. It outlines the questions you should ask and the way in which a strategy can be developed that will provide a clear-sighted route to help you to implement the approaches you have encountered in the book. By asking these questions and planning a simple strategy, you will be able to support your colleagues' informal learning activities in a way that has its foundations in your own understanding of your organization's situation, circumstances and purpose. Taking action will require effort from leaders and strategists; people concerned with performance and capability improvement and individuals who want to maintain and build their skills and competences. These questions, recipes and dos and don'ts work for all three groups.

Note

1 Cross, J (2007) *Informal Learning*, Pfeiffer, San Francisco, p 15.

SECTION ONE
Making sense of informal learning at work

This first section sets out an overview of informal learning. It seeks to define the terms that are applied to discussions of informal learning and to establish what role, if any, the organization can take in informal learning. In trying to make sense of what informal learning is – and what it isn't – you are also going to explore some models and processes. These are designed to help you critically to appraise alternative approaches that could support, or may hinder, employees' taking control of their own learning and capability improvement at work.

What is informal learning?

1

A lot of learning starts with stories, so let me tell you a story to help us get to grips with what informal learning might be.

Informal Learning is about doing different things and doing things differently

I like to bake bread. There is something incredibly satisfying about taking simple ingredients and creating something so elemental to the human diet.

A year or so ago I graduated from making dough rise by using a packet of dried yeast to the alchemical wonders of sourdough. It is a slow process. Incredibly, something that resembles failed wall paper paste, converts itself to a chewy, highly flavoured loaf that will last for days. I don't begin to understand all of the chemistry (or is it biology or even botany?) but I enjoy both the process and the results.

My first venture into sourdough came after I read a recipe in a magazine. I made some starter, a mix of flour and water, and left it to ferment. I fed it religiously as instructed and after the requisite delay, I incorporated it with more flour and water, salt and oil, and made bread. Or at least I made a loaf-shaped brick that could have been used as a blunt weapon. It got slightly better after a few attempts but its similarity to the output of the local artisanal bakery was limited to colour alone.

As many of us would, I consulted the internet to see where I was going wrong. What I found there were numerous blogs, articles and recipes that were all couched in the most positive of terms. 'It's so easy,' I was told. If you look to the internet to help solve a problem you will often be confronted with smiley, happy posts explaining how great/simple/

life-enhancing everything is. For the person struggling to do something new, this is the worst kind of advice – a digital reminder that you're a bit thick. I reached out (as the common parlance has it) to forums and community sites, but received no reply to my requests for guidance. Despite this, I was not to be defeated. I turned to old technology and bought a book, chucked out the old starter and made a new one (rye flour is the secret, if you're interested).

The independence of the informal learner

There are some universal elements of informal learning in my baking story:

- The learner was in control – determining both the what and the how;
- The learner set the objectives and standards in terms that were personally relevant;
- The process relied on experimentation, trial and error …
- … supported by resources and information from others;
- The approach was modified in the light of reflection about what worked and what didn't.

The process I went through was informal learning. It fulfilled the criteria of informal learning in that I had an entirely personal objective – no one else instructed me to make sourdough bread. In fact, those closest to me were quite satisfied with the traditional output and somewhat disadvantaged when I started to produce oven baked paving stones. I also went through a series of experiments and individual problem-solving activities to find out what might work. I chose to consult external sources of information and guidance to direct my efforts.

Through trial and error I determined a few rules about what worked and what didn't. The creation of my personal set of rules about sourdough bread production enabled me to replicate the more successful attempts. They also provided a reference point, something to go back to refine and revise as later versions were more successful. After about eight months I had started to turn out sourdough bread once a week that looked and, most importantly tasted, like something you might buy in a shop.

In some ways this was the pure form of informal learning. If I'd had the opportunity to learn at the elbow of someone with more experience, I may have picked up one way of working more quickly, but in truth I would have run the risk of being for ever bound to the way they did things. I could have become a slave to an established tradition.

The similarities with informal learning in other areas of endeavour are numerous. I was wholly in charge of what and why I wanted to learn something. Whether I was successful or not was determined wholly by my own perseverance and my own drive to master a craft. I chose the means by which I developed the knowledge and I planned when and how often I would practise the required skills. The standards I set, such as they were, were mine and mine alone. There was no external timetable or pressure to learn. If I learned, great, if I didn't – who cares? It was an example, in some respect, of informal learning that will be common to anyone with a hobby and it used a very traditional approach – a book and personal experimentation.

Learning to bake sourdough took some time. Other informal learning activities I've been involved in have had a deadline attached – such as learning Italian prior to going on holiday. But like many others, my attempt to improve my knowledge of the language floundered on its own deadline. Getting other things completed in time to allow me to board the plane diverted attention and once the holiday had happened, the need and motivation to learn faded into the background.

Assuming the motivation is there and the time is available, as Samuel Beckett put it, to 'Try again. Fail again. Fail better', anyone can learn using these approaches – occasionally with the requested input of someone who knows something they don't, occasionally as a solitary learner.

But I'm primarily interested in informal learning at work. At work, learning rarely happens like this and if it did, the elapsed time between interest and competence would be unacceptable for an organization. If I'm going to develop skills informally, I'd better aim to be a bit quicker in achieving something of benefit. If, as a learner, no one else cares about whether we learn something new or not, it can be difficult if not impossible to justify devoting any work time or effort to it – and certainly not a number of months on an ad hoc basis. If, as an organization, it doesn't matter how long someone takes to reach an acceptable level of competence, then the learning required will for ever be overtaken by events. Learning in organizations happens most effectively when there is a clear need and an immediate requirement to deploy the skills to be learned. The vagaries of my ability to commit time to improving my bread making or my ability to conduct a halting conversation in Italian would be of little use to an organization that depended on me mastering these skills.

A short history lesson

Informal learning has been with us since we first walked upright on the savannah. Our prehistoric ancestors didn't run sessions in the stone-age equivalent of the classroom. Throughout pre-history, hunter-gatherer people probably learned through watching what others did and taking increasing amounts of responsibility as they grew older, stronger and more capable.

We know that the kind of learning by imitation that we can assume that our ancestors used is not unique to humans. When macaque monkeys in Japan were fed by researchers, grain was spread on a sandy beach that the troupe visited regularly. The macaques were sufficiently dextrous to pick individual grains from the sand to eat. Shortly after, the troupe was observed copying the activities of one of their number. She put handfuls of the grain in the water at which point the grains floated to the surface and the sand sank to the bottom. This speeded up the process by which grains could be consumed and after a short while, the entire troupe had increased their efficiency by imitating this behaviour. Because individual macaque monkeys repeated this behaviour when the innovative matriarch was not present, this can clearly be described as learning.

Throughout much of history people needed to 'find things out' rather than 'be taught'. To some extent informal learning is the natural way of things. Looking at how 'finding things out' has happened may be instructive if we are to understand how and why informal learning works in modern organizations. Certainly, we can assert that we have always learned informally – through our own experience, by imitating others, by working out what worked and what didn't and by creating habits out of the behaviours that were most frequently successful.

On occasions we may have asked the advice of an elder or at least more experienced person in our circle. Occasionally, we will have been treated to the wisdom of others, whether we wanted it or not. Some people have always been free with their advice – whether they were using it or not.

In more hazardous situations, however, there is a risk associated with learning by doing and learning by imitation. When facing a large and injured animal that may be the source of food for the entire village for a week, having a novice getting in the way and potentially endangering themselves and others before allowing the prey to escape would probably have been considered a poor way of learning. This may be one of the reasons early humans prospered and were so much more successful than other primates. Their larger brains and longer childhood meant that stories and safe practice with peers could extend and add to imitation of the elders as a route to gaining capability.

There is a strand of thought that cave paintings, such as the famous ones at Lascaux in south-western France, had an instructive purpose alongside spiritual or ritual significance. Animals that were good to eat are portrayed with large bodies, skinny legs and small heads – the amount of meat gained from a successful hunt perhaps indicated by the distorted or emphasized proportions. Similarly, dangerous animals such as bears and wolves were depicted with disproportionately enlarged jaws and claws than in real life. This may have been advice handed from those with experience to those requiring knowledge. Maybe the cave paintings of hunter-gatherer civilizations were a kind of prehistoric PowerPoint. Perhaps, the natural learning through experience of our pre-historic ancestors was pre-empted by safe spaces to practise and more formal information giving.

Within later civilizations, we know that learning – certainly among adults – was undertaken through discussion. As reported by Plato and Xenophon, Socrates pioneered a dialectic method that has become known as Socratic questioning. Plato reported Socrates as saying 'The job of the educator is not to put knowledge where knowledge does not exist, but to turn the mind's eye to the light so it may see for itself.' In the Socratic method, or elenchus, learning is pursued through questions rather than by persuasion or instruction. It is a wholly oral tradition. In fact, Socrates is reported to have been somewhat against writing, preferring discussion and conversation as a route to truth.

The idea that elenchus, or the debates and discussions Socrates joined with in Athens, was what we would recognize as formal education is probably some way from the truth. Although somewhat more formal than a debate in the saloon bar of the Dog and Duck, it was some way distant from a lecture. More likely, the experience was akin to traditional Jewish scholars studying the Talmud in a Yeshiva, by endlessly debating each phrase and sentence to arrive at some level of understanding. The focus is on the student finding things out, in collaboration with their peers. This form of learning is not reliant on a teacher imparting his or her knowledge.

Apprentices and more structured preparation for work

If we fast forward 1,500 years to the 11th century we know that apprenticeships were evident in Turkey and by the 12th century this method of developing craft skills had spread to Europe. With a few differences, the apprenticeship system carried on pretty much as it always had done through until the post-war era.

My father was a post-war apprentice, starting to work for a Joinery business in 1947. To be an apprentice meant becoming 'indentured' – a contract between the employer and the apprentice's parents. My grandparents were obliged to supply my father's tools and to ensure that he was fed and housed and turned up each morning wearing the appropriate clothes.

In a slight change from the mediaeval period, my father was also required to attend night school, three nights and one whole day per week in the first year and thereafter four evenings a week until he was 21 years old. In this way the learning and knowledge were gained in two distinct ways. At college he would learn theory, mathematics, building regulations and the like. On the job, he would learn the practical skills. As he described it: 'They would show you once, perhaps twice if it was complicated or you hadn't picked it up first time. Then they'd watch you do it and then you were on your own.'

Practice pieces were designed to provide lower risk opportunities to learn. However, these were not solely for practice. Certainly in the joiner's shop where my father was apprenticed, the so-called apprentice pieces were expected to meet commercial standards and be sold to recover the costs of their creation. Jobs increased in complexity depending on the employer's increased expectations of the older apprentices. In this way different tasks were mastered and in a reinforcement of the learning process, a second-year apprentice might demonstrate the job he had recently mastered to his junior colleague.

During an apprenticeship, which could be as long as seven years, a young person would be exposed to tasks of increasing complexity. The output of each task was expected to meet the required standards. The traditional apprenticeship relied to a very large extent on a tradition of informal learning. Apprentices were given set tasks and a time by which to complete them and the instruction, 'If you don't know how to do something, ask!' The responsibility to develop capability was the learner's and the learner's alone. While it was in the interests of the firm to develop some apprentices, many were 'let go' at the end of the prescribed period and replaced by another school leaver who was cheaper, more biddable and under the control of his parents! Failure to learn quickly and to be able to perform at the required standard had a high price for the apprentice.

Academic development has always followed a similar path. There is a hangover from the times when university education and an apprenticeship with a craftsperson were fundamentally the same. Despite other breakthroughs in non-gender specific language, we still refer to graduates as having achieved bachelor status. Like an apprentice, studying was undertaken under the jurisdiction of a young person's parents and when they graduated, they became a bachelor – finally free to marry once they had completed their studies. The progression through masters to fellowship in universities takes a similarly supervised route to that experienced by craft apprentices. Research, learning by experience and experimentation, testing and proving or disproving hypotheses through questioning and argument owe as much to the apprenticeship system as to Socrates. Throughout our history we have relied on learning informally to develop the skills and knowledge required to make our way in the world. We have primarily learned *at* work by learning *through* work.

The work difference

The principal difference in learning at work compared to my baking or holiday language hobbyist learning is that, at work, the standards I need to meet are defined by others. Employers or clients should and do make demands on us to be competent and capable. Training departments may provide some inputs and programmes, but once we reach a certain level of experience and expertise we can't rely on the input of a separate function to keep our skills current. What's more, how can we expect an under-resourced and unfashionable team within human resources – that most maligned organizational department – to be able to predict all of our capability needs, months before we know what we need ourselves? We need to take control and become learners ourselves.

Throughout both my bread journey and my attempt to master rudimentary Italian, my motivation levels and application to the task of learning fluctuated wildly. Some days I was really focused, other days my planned activities were overtaken by events. Organizations cannot rely on such a fluctuating level of motivation for developing skills that are intrinsic to their future success.

In order for us to learn at work naturally, as we have through millennia, we need organizations to play a role in informal learning. If informal learning is to help to improve workplace capability it will need to be less ad hoc and less hit and miss than my attempts to bake bread or learn a language. My repeated, experimental failures would not have been tolerated if I was an apprentice, my fluctuating motivation would be a barrier to my engagement in Socratic dialogues. Research studies, often externally funded by those with an interest in the results, are conducted by doctoral students to a strict timetable. For informal learning to be applied at work, it will need to be organized. Standards will need to be established and communicated. Levels of capability will need to be defined against a timetable. Paradoxically, informal learning will need to become more formal.

The role of the organization in informal learning

My baking and language learning was informal learning, but too inefficient and hit and miss to be any use for a workplace. Academic learning and apprenticeships are necessarily rigorous. Experimentation and on-the-job learning plays a role but as an adjunct to a predominantly formal route from novice to mastery.

For informal learning to work within the efficient, rapidly changing and somewhat less predictable world of work, the organization needs to find new ways to support learners by:

- Providing a focus for the learning – why, what and when?;
- Inspiring, motivating and challenging the learner;
- Setting standards;
- Positively responding to aspirations; and
- Negotiating time frames.

A model of informal learning

2

I have spoken to many people involved in the business of improving workplace performance. From organizational development consultants to line managers to trainers and learning and development (L&D) strategists, each has their own idea of what makes informal learning work and each is slightly different. While trying to harness informal learning, there is an ambiguity about what the term actually means. This can be exceedingly useful to the commercial consultancy trying to tap into the current levels of perceived discontent with formal interventions. But being all things to everyone is not a route to clarity.

While thinking about what people had said and how we had learned since antiquity, I tried to develop a definition. I was after a pithy one liner, but in fact what emerged wasn't a definition but a model of how informal learning works (Figure 2.1).

If we explore the five stages of the model in more detail, we can see that the obvious start point is **observation**. Like the macaque monkeys sifting grains from the sandy beach we all, even as very young babies, observe what is going on around us and – having determined that this is a desirable trait or behaviour – we **imitate**.

Over time our imitation leads us to our own **experience**; a series of activities during which we develop our 'rules' of what works and what doesn't. This is the stage I've reached as a baker of sourdough bread as outlined in Chapter 1. Through my experience I don't slavishly copy what is being done by others, or the techniques explained in YouTube videos or in the pages of a book. I move beyond the imitation phase and put my own stamp onto what I'm doing. Once I have achieved the standard required – whether I established my own goals or these were set externally – I may stop there, my

FIGURE 2.1 An informal learning model

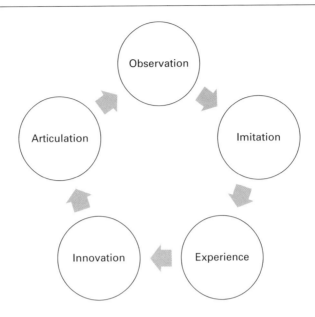

learning journey over, quite satisfied with what I've achieved. However, if I'm curious, driven, motivated – either intrinsically through my own targets or extrinsically by my employer because I will be promoted, paid more or simply recognized – I may **innovate**.

My innovation may be about doing completely new things, built on the foundations of my current, new-found capability. Alternatively, I may be engaged in incremental innovation – doing the same things faster or more efficiently. In any case, in a rapidly changing work environment, I may need to update and apply what I know in new contexts. Let's imagine I have learned double-entry bookkeeping. The advent of spreadsheets or accounting software doesn't render my skills and knowledge redundant – far from it. Knowing why a calculation may have gone wrong requires an understanding of the underlying logic. However, I'm unlikely to want to enter income and expenditure figures into a ledger once I have automated tools at my disposal. So I **innovate** and **combine**, synthesizing two capabilities – my approach to double-entry bookkeeping with all the tips and tricks I have incorporated into my practice over years of experience, and the use of a software tool. This gives me a new skillset.

Innovation may also be about simple problem-solving. This may not be new to the world. Simply new to you, but rather like my father at the age of 16 learning how to make doors, door frames and skirting boards, it could be about working out how to do something which no one has yet shown you how to do.

The final stage of the cycle is the **articulation** stage or **explanation**. This is the stage at which we may describe what we have done to others or set down our own manual for how we do things. In on-the-job learning, the use of reflective logs has become widespread. In effective examples of these logs, learners describe not just what was done but why, what happened and how it could have been different. The process of articulation is a spur to reflection. In the 21st-century hyper-connected world of work this explanation or articulation may take the form of a blog, a post on LinkedIn or a tweet. It will certainly form part of the discussion at the annual appraisal or performance review meeting.

If you are identified as having mastered a skill – like the master craftsmen and women of the apprenticeship systems of days gone by – then you may train others. In the apprenticeship system you became a master and were qualified and required to pass on your skills to your own apprentice in your turn. It was expected by communities that each skilled worker trained their own successor. It is a central plank of informal learning.

What do we mean by learning?

At this point it seems appropriate to define learning, regardless of the mechanisms used to achieve it. The definition I use is:

> Acquiring new or modifying existing knowledge, behaviours, skills, values, or preferences.

The key word in that sentence is 'acquiring'. For learning to have happened, it requires memory or competence – the learner 'owns' specific capabilities at the end of a learning process. The knowledge which may be acquired might be how to find information in the future – sources of future advice, guidance or information. This would seem to be consistent with the widespread belief that workers can no longer hold in their heads all the knowledge and information required to do their job. Being a skilled information seeker is a key 21st-century capability.

Alternatively, we could say that learning is analogous to a novice swimmer discarding their armbands. If a child requires a flotation device to get from one side of a swimming pool to the other, we can hardly describe them has having learned how to swim. At the stage of making an attempt across the pool without their armbands, we would hardly describe them as a fully competent swimmer, but they have acquired sufficient knowledge and skill to be able to swim. They have learned. In our world of ubiquitous connectivity there is a fine line between relying on the myriad sources of advice and information and being too scared to discard our intellectual armbands.

In organizational terms, an employee who needs to be constantly monitored, or who is limited in the jobs within their role which they are able to take on unsupervised, is clearly still learning. To move beyond this 'trainee' status, they need to be capable of completing all the jobs in their role profile, unaided, to an acceptable standard. As a first rule of supporting informal learning, an organization should start with defining what standards need to be achieved. Without a clear idea of what good looks like, any concept of competence is meaningless.

A definition of informal learning

Having got to my model, am I any closer to the pithy definition I sought? If I turn to learning and development teams I find little agreement. For some, informal learning is entirely directed and controlled by the learner. It absolutely, definitely must never have defined learning objectives and should happen naturally without direction – like my bread making. As I've said, this can't really be relied on to improve sufficiently the capability of employees. We need an alternative definition that encompasses a more reliable route to building capability.

Others would say informal learning is a by-product of the internet and the myriad opportunities to delegate our memory to our computers, the cloud or to search engines. The increased opportunity to collaborate with others in different locations, time zones and organizations provides all the motivation required to informally learn. Connectivity is an end in itself from which learning serendipitously flows.

For others informal learning is simply any activity during which learning happens but which doesn't involve being in a classroom or a training centre.

All these definitions seem rather exclusive to me. They are either/or choices. My experience of providing training and learning for individuals and groups is that binary choices are often predicated on false differences. People have a continuous and constant need to learn new things, master new skills, and adopt new behaviours. If we are to help them we need to be as open minded as possible. We need to recognize that the learning approaches that are available – and that people are most likely to use – could be as varied as those individuals whom we wish to help.

Looked at in this holistic way, to suggest that there is one type of informal learning and one way for it to be done would be silly. The truth is that there are many variations or degrees of informality. This variety may be best illustrated by Figure 2.2.

FIGURE 2.2 The informal/formal learning continuum

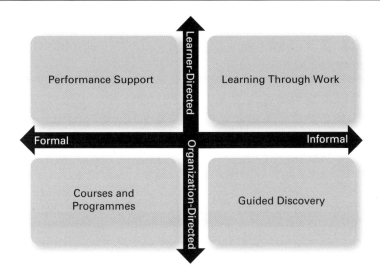

In the south-west quadrant we have traditional courses and programmes. By definition these are 'formal' learning interventions. But in reality this means we equate 'training' with 'learning'. If by learning we mean being able to do things differently and do different things, then classroom training alone is not going to work. Increasingly, apart from the rather blinkered organizations I described earlier, employers have recognized that using class-room courses as the sole mechanism for achieving new and more complex capabilities, is bound to deliver disappointment. True, some organizations only provide training through presentation-heavy classroom programmes but sometimes what happens during these sessions can barely be described as learning. In truth, what happens in these sessions is that the organization provides information, some of which may be retained by those in attend-ance. Those who are sufficiently motivated to try new things and new ways of working on the basis of such a session may do some self-directed learning through work on their return to the day job. In other words, where these sessions do work, they rely on a degree of informal learning taking place after the event to effect the required change in behaviour that improves performance.

In more and more organizations, those attending formal training programmes in the classroom or using eLearning programmes designed to address a required competence, are expected to do other things before and after their engagement with the formal instruction. The degree to which these initial, preparatory activities or follow up tasks are formal or informal depends on the degree to which these tasks are prescribed by the organization.

FIGURE 2.3 Performance support in the formal/informal learning continuum

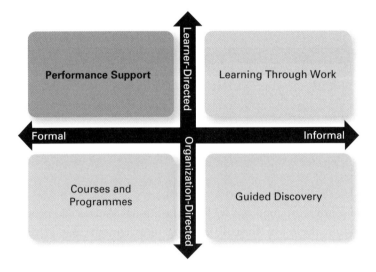

Above courses and programmes – in the north-west quadrant of Figure 2.3 – we have **performance support**. On occasions performance support tools are provided by the organization. These tools may include anything from help desks or FAQs or just-in-time learning assets. Perhaps they are as formal as mini-eLearning programmes which are typically designed to show you how to use the functions of a particular piece of software. In general terms, performance support tools provided by the organization, professional institute or by a software vendor are pretty formal. They exist as an extension of, or more often as an alternative to, the traditional course approach to teaching about procedures, tools or processes.

Increasingly, alongside pre-prepared tools, organizations will include access to experts or 'heroes'. This may include a forum in which a question may be posed or – in the more sophisticated instances – a community of practice.

Accessing these support tools and communities involves activities which are more akin to problem-solving. Many of us will have encountered a novel situation through our work. Perhaps it is new to us because of our relative inexperience or maybe it is a situation never before encountered by our organization or within the team or function in which we are employed. We need to do some hard thinking and try to find an approach which might work. Given that the majority of us have access to an unimaginably comprehensive library of information, resources and guidance, it is not unusual for us to use the simplest route to enlightenment. Yup, we google it!

What emerges from our search may be helpful. Alternatively, we may not know what we don't know and so we may be unable to make much headway by simply reading what others have chosen to make available. We may need guidance from others who have slightly more knowledge than us or are likely to have encountered similar situations in their own work. We could, therefore, turn to our networks for advice and use our connections – many of them mediated via social media – to assist us in problem-solving. Where we are genuinely solving a problem by synthesizing the available information, adapting it to our unique circumstances and combining disparate ideas with our own creativity to come up with new approaches to meet previously unmet challenges, then we are clearly learning. However, where we are simply asking someone for an answer which is provided by return tweet, then we may be able to achieve our goal without learning anything at all, beyond the fact that the person we asked knows how to do things which we don't.

In this quadrant, therefore, there are some genuine learning activities and some unreflective copying. That is not to say that copying what someone else has done is wrong. Imitation is one of the components of our informal learning model, after all. In circumstances where there is a simple answer to a question we are unlikely to face often in the future, looking something up or phoning a friend may be a perfectly reasonable tactic to enable us to get stuff done. But is it learning?

Copying the behaviour which a peer describes online is somewhat different. The behaviour is unobserved, merely described. This can make accurate imitation difficult. We will be required to experiment on our own. In some situations, time or inclination means we do not make the effort to work out the reasons why something was done in a particular way. This is most clearly experienced when trying to master a piece of software. A search of an FAQ list or a post on a forum is an obvious route to take if we don't understand how to manipulate an item of data in an Excel spreadsheet or create a fancy transition in some presentation software. By asking the question, hopefully we pick up a tip and implement it. Our immediate goal is achieved. But did we learn? That depends on whether we can replicate the activity in a few days', weeks' or months' time when we need to perform the same task again. If we need to repeat our search on the forum, then we can't be described as having learned. It was only through rapid and continuous repetition that the Japanese macaques mastered grain-washing. It may come as a shock but humans aren't that different from other primates. Unless we repeat, regularly and over a protracted period, we won't achieve mastery of the task we need to undertake.

The degree to which accessing forums and tools provided by our employers or partners are informal learning activities is dependent on the degree to which the learner is in control. When they are wholly directed by the individual learner, solving problems as and when needed, clearly these count as informal learning activities and fit with our model of observation, imitation and experience.

Looking things up – the **find, use and forget** model of seeking new information – is perfectly practical in a world in which things change quickly and in which it is difficult, if not impossible, to hold all the information we need to do our job in our heads. By anticipating the requirements of their workforce, organizations that provide performance support tools are attempting to ensure workers behave and perform in a particular way, to achieve specified tasks in order to meet a defined set of standards. They are also recognizing that a formal 'just in case' training course, covering – for example – every function of a piece of software, is unlikely to be retained unless it is used shortly after instruction, repeatedly and in order to achieve a task which is important to the individual. However, whether looking something up constitutes 'learning' in an accepted sense rather depends on whether or not the task can be accomplished in the future without reference to the support tool. If not, I would argue it is no more learning than using a set of instructions to assemble flat pack furniture. Despite many opportunities to develop my skills in assembling wardrobes I languish in a world of conscious incompetence. After decades of practice, all I have learned is don't – under any circumstances – lose the instructions!

Informal: guided discovery and learning through work

On the right of Figure 2.4 are the two quadrants I would describe as clearly informal learning. These are also the two areas which I find most interesting. **Guided discovery** encompasses everything from coaching to being asked to undertake preparatory activities before a formal course. It also includes

FIGURE 2.4 The informal components of the formal/informal
continuum

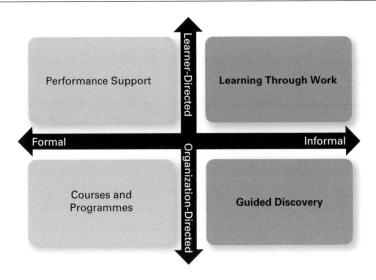

organized learning with peers. Working together, trying new things and reporting back on one's experiences to others who can provide additional insight. This involves reflecting on your own experience and enhancing it with new perspectives and stories. These interactions may happen spontaneously and be wholly directed by learners. However, for most of us the chance to collaborate, share and learn collectively will have been provided by our organization. Crucially, those participating will define what is to be shared and discussed based on their own needs and aspirations. Where an employer or external educational institution defines the content, this moves west to be closer to a formal programme or course.

The north-eastern quadrant is **learning through work**. One example would be an organization that provides a 'buddy system' in which an individual works alongside someone with more experience. The buddy will be charged with assisting when and where required. In this situation, the learning is rarely, if ever, one directional. The person being assisted learns 'how things get done round here'. By seeing their routines through new eyes, the person providing support may learn to question why things are done in the way they are. An old Russian proverb says that 'To teach is to learn twice'. Explaining things to a novice is a great way of re-learning, questioning and revising how we do what we do.

Learning through work also includes collaborative problem-solving and a more ad hoc sharing of experience. 'Working out loud' is a new buzz phrase. Rather than sharing an office with someone irritatingly explaining everything that they are doing – from going to the photocopier to opening up their packed lunch – this is meant to be an individual continuously reflecting on what works and what doesn't and sharing these reflections with others.

I should say that I am not convinced of the value of this to a third party. For this to be useful to someone else – or even just to make sense to a colleague – they would need to be working on similar if not the self-same problems and have similar needs and prior experiences. Without a clear understanding of one's own learning needs, others working out loud simply increases the level of background noise.

However, working out loud is of enormous benefit for the person articulating their experience. This is the articulation/explanation phase of the model for informal learning. Regardless of the learning mechanism or the degree of formality, reflection is an essential component of learning. Without reflection we do things, they work or they fail, and we have no way of knowing why. The difference between an experience and a learning experience is the degree to which we reflect on what happened, why it happened and the formulation of rules which we can apply to our future work.

At their most informal, these learning through work activities may be entirely unplanned and unanticipated. Perhaps these work activities are only revealed as learning after the event. Maybe the learning happens when the individual or group realizes that there could be a wider application of the experience they have been through. Novel experiences and the approaches, tools and action in which they were involved has led to them learning something new.

This gets to the heart of whether an experience properly can be described as learning. The degree to which the individuals involved are able to reflect, draw conclusions and plan future actions determines whether an activity constitutes learning. This is true regardless of the formality or informality of the learning approach. For learning to happen, reflection makes sense of our experiences – whether these involve sitting in a lecture hall, working as part of a project team or linking up with our peers via Twitter.

Informal = better?

There's a widespread belief that informal learning is somehow better, more natural. It is regularly described as much more effective than the 'imposition' of classroom courses. Formal learning is routinely described as being unfit for purpose in the modern workplace.

Going back to the four quadrants of the informal learning continuum, where each box touches or perhaps overlaps is where the opportunities lie to execute strategies for increasing and improving informal learning in organizations. These are also the areas where organizational decision makers – those in charge of the strategic direction of their organization – should pay greatest attention. Those overlaps and the activities, risks and opportunities that can only happen in the spaces between one activity and the next is where good practice lives and what this book is about.

In the next chapter I'll be looking at the capability contract. In some instances this is written down – a detailed requirement which the organization demands of the individual to maintain their skills and knowledge. In other situations this is an implied requirement, a loose set of expectations which differentiate the organization's sheep from their goats.

Whether formally outlined or informally expected it is a truism that change is a constant and organizations expect their individual employees to take significant responsibility for ensuring their skills are fit for purpose. In industries in which there has been the most profound change in recent times, informal learning has been examined thoroughly and the starting point is that good old learning and development standpoint: 'What skills do we actually need people to have in 21st-century organizations?'

The capability contract

3

Work is hard, probably, harder than it's ever been. Not physically – those of us engaged in physical work where we use our brawn and stamina and strength are aided now by tools and equipment the like of which our predecessors could only wonder at. Lifting, carrying and man-oeuvring things into place are still strenuous and tiring activities, but no more so than in previous times. As workers, we are expected to keep our-selves fit, and to update our health and safety awareness, but with the excep-tion of new procedures and processes, our capability contract – that is, our responsibility for maintaining a set of skills that are fit for the organization's purpose – is understood and pretty straightforward.

Routine work in factories has been automated and mechanized beyond recognition. The daily grind of the assembly line and the packing room may be wearing by the repetitiveness of its nature, but it hasn't got harder since Henry Ford first created the production line around a century ago. Once again our capability contract is simple enough. Keep safe, maintain our awareness of procedures and be on top of the skills required to achieve pro-duction targets.

But brain work is different. We may be discussing a 'white collar factory' – the contact centre or data-processing office that has been automated along the lines of the Taylorist production lines of the dawn of the 20th century. Alternatively, we may be talking about office environments peopled by knowledge workers, creatives or strategists. Whichever, the work in these environments has reached what we might describe as 'peak memory'. In other words, the capability contract here has exceeded our individual capacity. Work is so much more complex than once it was that we can no longer hold in our heads the myriad of information, processes, regulations and rules to be able to perform our jobs based on our memory alone. We need to be able to look things up.

In these environments, being a skilled information seeker is **the** 21st-century requirement. Consulting manuals, job aids and the internet is now a daily occurrence for those primarily employed for their knowledge. From retail assistants expected to know significant levels of detail about thousands of product lines to physicians required to have an encyclopaedic understanding of different drug therapies, this knowledge work is not limited to those working in offices.

The pace of change in the world of work has accelerated. When I started my working life, the remainder of the floor of the office block in which I was based housed the typing pool. Letters were drafted longhand, then submitted for typing. Up to a week later, my letters were despatched over the signature of the director responsible for my department. For the most part, those kinds of letters are now automated – standard letters or blocks of text selected from a menu. The correspondence assembly line of the typing pool has also been automated.

When I first designed eLearning programmes, many organizations could not take advantage because access to the internet was banned within workplaces. Concerns about computer viruses, pornography downloads or time spent shopping online were cited as reasons. In the days of dial-up internet connections, the costs of being online were considered too expensive to enable access to the information available in the web's early days. On one occasion an eLearning programme I designed was rolled out to car dealerships for sales people to use. The programme failed dismally because the only internet-enabled computer was usually found in the dealer principal's office or on the desk of the sales manager. The novice sales person for whom the programme was designed was rarely allowed access.

Overall, the knowledge worker's life has been made easier by ubiquitous web access. But on another level, it has also led to unimaginable and unmanageable complexity. Peter Drucker once said: 'In order to do something new, you have to stop doing something old.' The web has enabled us to do lots of new things, without removing much of the old stuff from the agenda.

Continuing professional development

In certain roles, there has always been a written requirement for those practising the profession to maintain their capability. Continuing professional development, or CPD, has long been an ingredient in the working lives of teachers, doctors, lawyers and other professional roles. The idea of constant change is balanced by the need for individuals to keep themselves abreast of those changes. This updating has been a contractual obligation, a requirement to maintain standards and to undertake and document the activities that the individual engages in in order to maintain competence and continue to practise.

According to the Chartered Institute of Personnel and Development (CIPD), the UK-based organization representing those working in human resources, CPD should be:[1]

- continuous – professionals should always be looking for ways to improve performance;
- the responsibility of the individual learner to own and manage;
- driven by the learning needs and development of the individual;
- evaluative rather than descriptive of what has taken place;
- an essential component of professional and personal life, never an optional extra.

The key components of this checklist would certainly position much of what is described as CPD within the arena of informal learning. Learners owning and managing their development driven by their individual needs, appears to be a description of high-quality, informal learning activities.

In reality however, some CPD is often a process of ticking a box – professionals completing a bare minimum of activities to gain the required 'points' to enable them to fulfil the arduous responsibility of maintaining their licence to continue in their profession. In jobs that are not supported by CPD, **Personal development plans** or PDPs are often agreed annually at appraisal time. Again, they are informed by standards such as internal competence frameworks or job profiles. However, these too are no guarantee of good practice. All of us who work in learning and development can tell stories of the PDP process being reduced to the most inane of box ticking procedures, simply to 'keep HR off the line manager's back'.

This is not to denigrate all PDPs or CPD, merely to question whether everything that professionals do to keep their skills current is recorded – or recordable – and whether this is the core of their continued professional updating. It could be argued that even where the requirement for CPD points accumulation is primarily a bureaucratic process, it still serves a purpose. Even as an exercise in form filling, it ensures that individual practitioners understand the need to maintain their competence and that this requires specifically designed activities that can be audited, recorded and measured.

FIGURE 3.1 Kolb's learning cycle

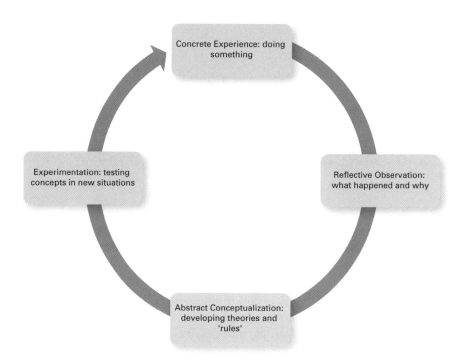

Many CPD frameworks have started to move beyond simply defining a list of eligible activities. The General Pharmaceutical Council (GPhC) is the independent regulator for pharmacists, pharmacy technicians and pharmacy premises in Great Britain. Its CPD framework,[2] revised in 2014, is based on Kolb's learning cycle (see Figure 3.1).

A practising pharmacist, pharmacy technician or pharmacy manager will need to log nine CPD activities per year. Of these, three will need to start with reflection – that is, reflecting on current practice or thinking about a live issue or a recent work related event. The pharmacist plans what they need to learn and how they intend to plug any knowledge or skills gaps. They need to document what has happened, complete their plan and evaluate its effectiveness against the goals they set as a result of their reflective thinking.

The mechanisms that pharmacists are expected to use do not exclude formal courses. Quite the contrary, a reflection by a pharmacist might be that she needs to learn about a new drug treatment and the most efficient way of doing so could be to attend a course or complete an eLearning programme. However, the implication of prioritizing the reflective process as the main tool for learning places the legal obligation to continually develop skills and knowledge firmly in the informal realm. As independent practitioners, pharmacists are expected to take control of their learning and formulate their own plans, against their own timetable, to ensure they are sufficiently updated.

This anticipated independent proactivity is the start to any informal learning journey. Under the terms of the GPhC's continuing professional development requirements, for at least one third of all learning activities logged during a year, the start point is the individual reflecting on their experiences, requirements for the future and current capabilities, and using the outcome of those reflections as the basis for planning their subsequent learning. Not only that, but for a pharmacist – as with many professions – it is a legal requirement that they complete the necessary CPD to the standards laid down by their professional and regulatory body. Not to complete their CPD is not an option. It would lead to the individual no longer being able to practise their profession.

For a pharmacist or a physician, failure to keep up to date may have extremely serious consequences for patients. For architects or civil engineers, the continued security of the buildings and highways they design requires a similarly robust approach to assuring competence.

In jobs outside the CPD-regulated professions, the capability contract is not necessarily written down and signed by employee or employer. It is a requirement to which those working with knowledge tacitly accede. As the CIPD has described, keeping one's knowledge and skills current is not an optional extra. It is a prerequisite of continued employment. Organizations and industries that embrace continuous updating without recourse to a mandatory framework need to adopt a culture in which change is recognized as a constant and the need to update skills and knowledge accepted as part of the day-to-day work.

If we want people to be continuously capable in a rapidly changing work environment, then we can learn from those professions who have the power of the law behind their efforts to ensure continuous learning. In these professions, there is a culture that supports and enables learning. More than that, those organizations employing professionals governed by CPD recognize that their professional employees have a right to time for training, time to reflect on their development needs and time to plan activity to meet those needs. The capability contract includes rights and responsibilities on both sides. Those employers who voluntarily institute personal development plans and similar measures to keep employee's skills and knowledge on the work agenda require a culture in which learning is commonplace, natural and not 'other'.

Vocational qualifications

One halfway house between a more ad hoc approach and the obligatory updating of mandatory continuous professional development is found in the introduction of in-work qualifications. In the UK, the National Vocational Qualifications (NVQ) process has been superseded by the Qualifications and Credit Framework Agency (QCF).[3] Among other things, this agency seeks to establish equivalence between different qualifications so that employers and further and higher educational establishments are able to compare one with the other.

Traditionally, national vocational qualifications relied on learners seeking evidence of competence. Ideally this evidence was generated through day-to-day activities, backed up by supervisor endorsements or by artefacts of capability generated through the work itself. The role of the Sector Skills Councils – representing the industries for which qualifications are required – aimed to maintain this link between on-the-job competence and demonstrated in-work capability and the qualifications that individuals achieved. That was the theory in any case.

All vocational qualifications are designed for generic job roles and – despite the involvement of employers – these roles rarely exist. It is inevitable that for many workers, their individual job roles are only an approximate fit to the role as defined within the qualification specification. The QCF drive for equivalence, that academic and vocational qualifications at the same level can be compared regardless of subject, means that the requirement of the workplace is no longer the only consideration when designing qualification outcomes nor the assessment mechanisms.

Knowledge or skills?

As a consequence of these two different drivers, some of the tasks anticipated in the competences and capabilities defined by the qualification are not activities that routinely appear on a worker's to do list, particularly if they are relatively new to the role. To make these qualifications work and to ensure that all candidates have achieved the required competence some outcomes that are not demonstrated on the job have been placed into the QCF assessment criteria. The problem is these specific assessment tasks – which do not reflect the actual work done – require assignments to be completed that are similar to academic qualifications rather than ones designed to enable a demonstration of work-based qualifications. These assessments measure what people know rather than what they can do. These assessment tasks may be perceived as being easier and cheaper to administer than on-the-job observations of competence. As a result they have become the default assessment mechanisms for vocational qualification.

Let's consider someone learning to be an electrician. Knowing how to isolate a circuit from the mains electric is a pretty important initial stage of the learning process. This is underpinning knowledge that may just keep the learner alive.

But being able to describe how it is done in a written assignment during which time the learner will have access to Google and YouTube is somewhat different from being able to carry out the process in a home or factory. Work flow learning enthusiasts with a technological bent will argue that with the ubiquity of smartphones, access to the information via an app or via the internet is perfectly reasonable and an effective alternative to carrying this kind of information around in one's head. They may have a point.

However, in the process of gaining a qualification, our fictional electrician gains a degree of confidence in their abilities that may mean that when faced with an unfamiliar junction box they rely on what their qualifications tell them they ought to know. Without the practical skills having been assessed in a real work environment, the protocols and safe working practices may not be embedded or habitual. Rather than taking the time out to consult the available information and advice, however this may be provided, they might just rely on a sketchy recollection of the information they cut and pasted into a written assignment some months earlier. If this recollection is less than perfect, any error could be pretty costly.

In many roles, there is a clear requirement for workers to demonstrate their knowledge of key pieces of legislation or the theory of why something works. This kind of knowledge based assessment is fine – so long as it is accompanied by, and supportive of, an assessment of skills performed in a work environment.

Now I'm sure that electricians are regularly assessed as competent through being observed carrying out real jobs in real situations. But to run a proper work based qualification that certifies competence in a job, an organization needs a team of assessors in place. These individuals should visit each candidate and observe them in their workplace, speak to line managers and supervisors and check that the evidence gathered meets the specifications. It is a time-consuming process and can only be undertaken by an experienced and well-qualified individual. In some industries, where there is an expectation that all staff will have achieved, or be working towards, a recognized qualification at a defined level, the temptation to streamline evidence gathering and assessment activities is understandable. Where that streamlining removes observation and oversight in the work-place, then inevitably the qualifications will be much weaker.

It seems to me that this is not the vision that was first outlined when I was involved in delivering the original NVQs almost 30 years ago. In those days, the focus was on proven capability not by submitting a written assignment but by producing something that demonstrated competence. Where a physical product was not available – for example in a customer service role or similar – the individual was observed by his or her line manager and both candidate and observer wrote a brief report of what had happened and how the trainee had demonstrated that they achieved the defined competence. This was double checked and endorsed by an independent assessor observing a subsequent example of activity and signing off the account provided by those at the sharp end. It was a time-consuming process as any certification activity with a degree of independence and rigour is wont to be.

Most importantly, this approach to proving capability located the learning activity leading up to the achievement of competence in the realm of day-to-day work. It required not only the identification of 'good' but its performance as well. What formal instruction was provided quickly gave way to on-the-job experience: observation, action, feedback, reflection and improvement. At its core it was the very best kind of informal learning in organizations. It was focused on achieving an agreed, externally defined standard and it relied on practical experience rooted firmly in the job at hand.

The experience of some workers undertaking the modern day vocational qualifications contrasts quite significantly with those initial days of observation based accreditation. The learning that does happen is often located somewhere other than in the work flow. Pressure on staff time and the requirements of external regulators can lead to situations where gaining the qualification matters significantly more than undertaking the required learning or demonstrating the required competence. The temptation to reduce the exercise to a series of boxes to be ticked and forms to be filled could be – and perhaps is – irresistible.

This doesn't mean that informal learning does not go on. But I would argue that work-based informal learning is ineffective as a means of delivering certifiable competence unless supported by clear, well understood and relevant standards. Developing basic job related skills absolutely requires on-the-job practice, support from peers – especially those who have more experience – and oversight by those with the skills to provide feedback, hints and tips for improvement and, where required, assurance that the individual is competent to undertake the required job.

When I was first involved in delivering vocational training, the workshop I managed had some machinery that was outside the scope of the qualifications any trainees were working towards. We felt it was important that these trainees should have experience of using this machinery before being considered competent. My colleagues and I introduced a system borrowed from other safety conscious industries called Permit to Operate. Each individual was issued with an in-house certification booklet that included a page for each machine in the workshop. Alongside this were four simple stages:

- observation of use;
- use under instruction;
- use under supervision;
- demonstrated safe use.

At each of these stages, the trainee and his or her supervisor would date and sign each stage. The Permit to Operate was completed and validated only once the trainee had used the machine under instruction on two occasions and used the machine under supervision on three occasions. The final stage required them to show someone that they knew how to use the equipment without damaging the expensive kit and without getting their fingers, hair or overalls tangled in the moving parts. All workshop supervisors and some senior team members had been formally trained in providing instruction on machine use and in safely supervising new starters as they first used the machines.

(*Continues*)

> This simple certification created a culture of gradual improvement. It supported a natural graduation from formal training to informal learning. It also created a culture of safe working in the workshop. After the introduction of the Permit to Operate the number of reportable accidents in the workshop was reduced to zero over a 12-month period.

Learning together

The conclusions I draw from looking at work-based qualifications, PDPs and CPD is that the existing culture needs to be conducive to this learning before a degree of self-managed, informal learning can really be effective. The organization has a requirement to create the environment in which learners can learn from their peers and can take responsibility for updating their own skills and knowledge. Even where individuals are not part of a large organization, learners are helped by a similar culture that expects professionals to continually learn and develop their practice. The CPD process as followed by the GPhC covers a large number of pharmacists who work in small shops where they may be the only professional in the building. By being part of the governing body's professional standards, the learning is located within the wider professional community. Although each individual is responsible for maintaining their own capability – and amassing sufficient points to measure the extent to which they have kept their skills and knowledge current – every other pharmacist and pharmacy is part of the same process and every other high street dispensing chemist is following the exact same steps.

In those organizations where personal development planning has been introduced (and is taken seriously by line managers and team members) then the existence of competency frameworks or role profiles can replicate the CPD system and similarly create a culture of standards-based, continuous learning.

Vocational qualifications can also introduce learners to informal learning and becoming independent learners in the workplace. It seems to me that the formal programme is a prerequisite. Whether that requires off-the-job training courses is a moot point. It may be perfectly possible to locate both the learning and the gathering of evidence of demonstrable capability within the day-to-day work undertaken by an individual. Vocational qualifications should, though, require candidates to demonstrate their capability through work based tasks. When used in this way, vocational qualifications present an exciting and interesting approach for the introduction of more informal learning activities based on observation, imitation, experience and articulation.

CASE STUDY NG Bailey

NG Bailey is the UK's largest independent engineering, construction, IT and facilities services business. Its infrastructure projects include major retail developments, railway stations and power plants. The company employs over 2,600 people in five different divisions – engineering, IT Services, rail, offsite manufacture and facilities services.

For many years, NG Bailey has been a leading provider of apprenticeships. As with apprenticeships of days gone by, modern day apprentices rely on a certain amount of informal learning to address practical skills training and also to provide opportunities to demonstrate their understanding of any necessary underpinning knowledge – whether that is mathematics, regulations or working safely.

The challenge with being recognized as a provider of high quality apprenticeships within an industry is that other employers can find a relatively rapid route to gaining the same skills that a company like NG Bailey has invested in developing. From recruiting school leavers with the potential to succeed to funding training courses, providing supervisors and conducting on-the-job assessments, apprentice training is not a cheap option when it's done right. It is a much more economically advantageous route to poach those workers who have already been trained at someone else's expense by offering slightly more money, perks and benefits such as international travel or a fast track route to promotion.

This was the challenge that Frank Clayton, NG Bailey's group head of learning and development faced when he was investigating how best to retain talent. Retaining skilled people became a particularly pressing issue when the market for major infrastructure projects started to pick up again after the economic downturn of 2008. As Frank told me: 'We saw the market start to turn a corner and – like many organizations – we had slightly reduced our apprenticeship intake during the previous years. When the industry started to look up, it became even more crucial that we held on to the people we had trained, and we faced more competition for good, well trained people as the whole industry started to gear itself up for new opportunities.'

Frank's obvious start point was to look at the talent management process in the business and what he found had room for improvement. 'We had an annual list of people who were considered "talent" but no ongoing process. In fact, we had a number of lists. People who were identified as having potential one year were then given more challenging roles and, as a result, fell back in relation to some of their peers. The first step in improving the talent development process was to develop a global list of those with high potential, that is, those deemed capable of being promoted to a position two levels higher than the one they currently occupied. The global talent list extended to those with advanced capability who, with the right sort of development, were ready to move into a more demanding role one level higher.'

In speaking to Frank, what I found really interesting about the talent management process is that it was all encompassing. Those completing an apprenticeship were also included. As Frank told me: 'The end of an apprenticeship is the start of a career journey, not the end of something.' The group learning and development team was looking to develop apprentices who had the credibility and ability to lead teams and work with colleagues in different settings. This was identified as being particularly important in the many joint ventures in which NG Bailey was involved. Workers who had only recently completed their apprenticeship were expected to be able to fulfil their trade role and act as an ambassador for the company in joint venture teams. These typically bring together the skills and expertise of several different companies.

One informal route to developing the confidence to represent the company was to give apprentices a role in NG Bailey's schools outreach programme, Inspire. Apprentices who may have only recently left school were expected to speak to students about career opportunities in the field of engineering and infrastructure. The benefits in building communication skills and confidence in speaking in public were instantly realized. 'We have a number of staff embedded in client organizations. Problem-solving, communication and working in a team are crucial skills. The trade skills need to be complemented by soft skills, team skills and customer service. We engage in 360 degree reviews of the capabilities of each individual apprentice. Apprenticeships are the start of our talent pipeline.'

As with many workplaces, employees who are due to be promoted will often move into jobs in which managing others is a central part of the new role. Frank's own assessment of the management style most often employed across the industry was one that was very hierarchical – a 'command and control' management style. As the industry changed, the projects became more complex and more partnership based and this top down management approach was seen as being somewhat outdated.

The challenges facing Frank Clayton and his team were quite clear:

1 Keep trained and talented staff working in the organization by creating a clear path for career advancement;

2 Prepare these staff to undertake management and supervisory roles in a much more complex environment than had previously existed; and

3 Influence the culture of management across the organization to be more appropriate for a 21st-century organization working as a trusted partner with its supply chain, project partners and clients.

It's fair to conclude that these were challenges that were easier to articulate than they were to address.

I often advise organizations to stick close to what they know how to do and Frank Clayton and his team recognized that they were pretty good at delivering qualifications for apprentices. It will come as no surprise that they chose another qualification route to meet the three challenges they now faced.

Employees identified as having advanced capability were offered the chance to complete a leadership course provided under the auspices of the Institute of Leadership and Management. The course is a level five programme, roughly equivalent to a University degree, and runs for between 18 months and two years. Over the course of the programme, formal delivery is limited to seven or eight sessions that each last two or three days. These formal inputs provide the basis for informal learning to take place.

Most importantly, the informal learning in between the workshop sessions is where the challenges Frank and his team outlined were most likely to be met. One key activity designed to encourage the kind of skills and mind-set required to learn informally was through the provision of coaching. In a smart move, NG Bailey partnered with 'PB Coaching', an organization that provides a range of coaching, leadership and organizational development programmes and that also works with Leeds Beckett University delivering coaching courses accredited at senior practitioner level by the European Mentoring and Coaching Council (EMCC). The coaches working with the NG Bailey team were students on PB Coaching and Leeds Beckett University's post-graduate certificate in executive and business coaching.

John Crossan is a member of the PB Coaching team and he explained that each of the trainee coaches on this programme needs to undertake a number of hours of coaching to gain the EMCC accreditation. The partnership with NG Bailey provided a number of his students with the opportunity to gain experience and provided the firm with a pool of coaches to match with their people.

As well as coaching sessions, each NG Bailey participant also took part in an action-learning set and undertook a project. John Crossan saw the coaching as a key enabler of these two activities.

'In our approach to coaching, the aim is lasting behavioural change. After an initial contracting phase where we establish the overall organizational and individual objectives of the coaching, we need to raise awareness of the here and now, all the challenges and opportunities, what they are thinking, their values and feelings. We encourage the person being coached to take greater responsibility for their own behaviours and their own performance. It's very important that each session features a mini-goal – brought by the coachee. The coach's job is to help the client identify the key challenges to be overcome in order to meet the goal,' John told me. He went on: 'It's also important that the goal is neither too ambitious nor too easy. If it is too easy they'll find that they have bitten off too little and stay hungry.'

This two-pronged solution is so simple and yet I have rarely heard of anything similar in organizations seeking to encourage informal learning. In order to learn independently and be responsible for one's own skills and development, each worker must take responsibility for what they need to learn and how they will learn it. Making a commitment – a contract – with an external coach is a recognized way of engendering that ownership of one's development. Senior executives who have used external coaches for many years all know this, but the really ingenious approach here was to simultaneously help trainee coaches to develop and practise their skills, experience new challenges and reflect on their own approach.

'Each of our trainee coaches is required to keep a reflective journal. Note taking during the session can potentially disrupt the "contact" – that's a key feature of the Gestalt approach we adopt in our practice. But after each session the coach should make notes and reflect on the process and also the relationship,' John explained. 'At the start of subsequent sessions, coaches need to take time to land. 15 minutes in the room before the coaching session commences, a chance to read the notes, reflect on what happened last time and be prepared for the session to come.'

As well as their own notes and reflections each coach has a series of supervision sessions that provide additional insights into their own learning and the learning still required.

When I spoke to a number of participants in the level five leadership programme, I started by asking about the coaching.

Chris McGrath is a project manager based in NG Bailey's Manchester office. An apprentice trained electrician he has moved by stages into project management that involves everything from bid management to delivering the project to the client on time and on budget.

'The coaching was superb. I build a new team for each project and that can be 20 to 30 people including sub-contractors, suppliers and all the different trades needed on the job. For our own people it's really important to keep them motivated and our personal development plans are one of the ways of doing that. By using some of the coaching techniques I learned I've been able to keep people focused. Previously, personal development plans had been de-motivational. The use of coaching enabled me to agree clear goals and follow through. One guy needed a new skillset that was quite innovative. There was no course available, so he needed to be seconded to another division of the business for a while. He'd previously been disengaged but because I followed through and helped him to arrange that secondment, he felt valued.'

Andy Bones is a design engineer, also based in NG Bailey's Manchester office. He agreed that the coaching had provided a model of behaviour he could seek to imitate. 'The coaching really added value. It means I take more notice of other people. There's quite a lot of pressure, we work under constant deadlines. I used what I've learned to help people feel valued. I needed to recognize their values and their drivers and respond to them.'

Andrea Efstathiou is a technical development manager working in NG Bailey's specialist IT services division. 'I tend to mentor quite a bit. I've tried to use the coaching approaches that we experienced. What I've realized is that if you just tell people things, it doesn't stick. If they work it out themselves, it sticks.'

As well as being coached about coaching, the course participants were also involved in a number of reflective assignments and their own projects. These were discussed in both the coaching sessions and in Action Learning Sets (ALS). The ALS were self-administered, sub-groups of the cohort that met together in between sessions, discussing specific assignments and progress towards learning goals.

Gemma Novo is a management accountant based in London who has been with NG Bailey for six and a half years, having originally joined on the company's graduate scheme. 'The action learning sets have been useful, as it is beneficial to spend time together with people across the business. It provides context, especially operationally and I gained insights into the challenges that others face.'

Chris added: 'It's really interesting to hear others talk about how they've addressed issues, completed the assignments and tried things out. It's important to know when to challenge and to have the confidence to be controversial when you need to be.'

Andy was equally enthused by working collaboratively with his peers: 'It's very informal. But they do provide an opportunity to reflect on what you've found out and your own experiences. It's a chance for everyone to reflect and to have their reflections critiqued by others.'

Andrea tends to work alone, both providing technology support and preparing the business for the future by trend spotting new technology innovations on the horizon. As someone who is not usually involved in a regular team the ALS presents him with a different view point. 'The course gave us the building blocks but not the whole or only answer. We need to take those tools and do some of our own digging. The more tools you have the better you can do the job. By talking things through with others who are dealing with these concepts for the first time as well, you can put your own stamp on it.'

As Frank Clayton said in my initial interview with him: 'We wanted to hold up a mirror to people, help them to answer the question "What do I need to do to develop?".' It seems to me that this is a prerequisite for organizations wanting to harness the opportunity and power of informal learning.

Frank would love the action-learning sets to continue after the level five programme has ended. I'm not sure that this will happen although I sincerely hope it does. The benefits of these peer supported learning discussions are too important not to be sustained, but their continuation may need other inputs if they are to flourish in a busy, highly pressured environment.

Conclusions

If we look at the process of enabling a learning culture to develop and to enable the organization to meet its side of the capability contract, it's pretty clear to me that there are three things that should be in place:

1 Some standards that are clear and easily understandable and that people can use to review their own performance and identify where they need new skills, new knowledge or more experience. The standards also provide a goal to be reached and an expectation that the updating of knowledge and skills is not an added extra but integral to the work.

2 Structures that encourage people to try things out on the job and be supported while these new work practices are in their infancy. Learners need someone to turn to, someone to bounce ideas off and someone to provide feedback. As we saw from John Crossan's approach to coaching, they also need to tell someone else what they are aiming to learn. The development journey needs to start from a series of public commitments.

3 Groups that work together need more in common than the artificial and time limited connection of being enrolled on the same programme. As we saw with the pharmacists and with the engineers, meeting those in similar disciplines provides lots of opportunity for common ground and common learning. But as we also saw with the

management accountant, meeting with others from other functions is unlikely to be prioritized in the face of competing demands from a stressful, intense workload.

Above all, the capability contract requires each of us to be aware of workplace changes, new trends, new technologies and amended legislation. This awareness needs matching with a preparedness to embrace the changes and learn and develop new skills. But this drive for development will not just happen. Busy people need to be encouraged, instructed or enabled to learn and organizations that sit back and expect it to happen without structures, resources and direction are likely to be extremely disappointed.

Developing a systematic approach to helping teams and individuals to learn in a way that meets their needs and aspirations, is where we are headed next.

Notes

1 Marchington, M and Wilkinson, A (2006) *Human Resource Management at Work (People Management & Development)*, 3rd edn, CIPD3, London.

2 General Pharmaceutical Council (2014) *Plan and Record: A guide to the GPhC's requirements for undertaking and recording continuing professional development*, version ii (revised April 2014).

3 Accredited Qualifications (2012) Qualifications and Credit Framework (QCF), available at http://www.accreditedqualifications.org.uk/qualifications-and-credit-framework-qcf.html [accessed 30 May 2015].

Formal training and the budget paradox

4

As NG Bailey found, certain types of informal learning require a kick-start. Individuals taking responsibility for developing their own work skills doesn't happen in most organizations just by chance. At least, not if one is interested in informal learning that supports organizational strategy. The improvement of crucial capabilities needs plans, platforms and programmes to encourage development in the right direction.

For sure, there will be a few people who will be enthusiastic about sucking all available input and building their skills and knowledge. My experience of these individuals also includes a fair few who are interested in building their CV as well, each job a step on a ladder to the kind of salary and status they were born to command. Even with these avid corporate mark makers, they are not necessarily informally developing their skills in the direction the organization would want. If we look at certain firms in, for example, banking, perhaps there is evidence that what was learned informally by the thrusting and ambitious was some distance away from the strategic interests of their employers.

However, engagement in managing informal learning is not on the radar of L&D teams in some organizations. In these businesses training and learning are considered synonymous, even though, as I illustrated in the introduction, quite a lot of what goes on in corporate classrooms cannot be labelled as training, let alone learning. Not only is 'learning' considered to be the same as attending courses or completing mandatory multimedia modules served up by the learning management system, it is quite definitely someone else's job.

For many years I worked with a global fast moving consumer goods company that prided itself on its coaching culture. New recruits were enticed to apply by the continuous focus on personal development paraded across its corporate web pages. The company's employer brand talked of support for learning and of the high performance teams created by the relentless feedback. (This feedback was described as the breakfast of champions at one point. No cliché left behind.)

When I instituted a project with the sales and marketing teams in the organization, my team and I were surprised to see lower than expected take up of the programmes and materials produced. Each module included eLearning, materials to support team based sessions, coaching notes and guidance and – should they be required – full workshop programmes to support those for whom access to the online modules in English was not appropriate.

Having found that few, if any, line managers were downloading the coaching guides we undertook a survey of more than 2,500 people including over 700 team leaders and line managers. This survey found that a sizable minority, around 40 per cent, believed that 'coaching should be the job of the HR team' and 'we do not have any time to undertake coaching sessions with our team members'.

The self-service approach to supporting line managers in their role as builders of team capability foundered on the rocky shore of reality. Training, development and managing learning were not activities considered to be part of their job by a significant proportion of team leaders. Senior staff believed differently. They thought line managers should be undertaking development activities through team meetings and regular one-to-one coaching and feedback sessions. But, crucially, they did not factor the time required to do these tasks into their staff planning. In sales teams that were target driven and responsible for meeting revenue and profit targets in each territory, the team leader was also expected to be top sales person and key account manager. Coaching others, while so operationally involved, was never going to be a priority. When new members joined the team there was an expectation of time spent bringing them up to speed. We followed up the survey results with observations and discussions and found that at best, induction was focused around watching the sales manager perform his or her client management tasks, with an expectation that the new joiner would amass a set of skills and behaviours through some kind of sales osmosis.

It may seem like I'm being particularly harsh on this organization. However, the reason I haven't named them is because they deserve no opprobrium. In my experience you could say pretty much the same thing about every large organization with teams based in remote territories. The diktats that emanate from global headquarters about continuous learning rarely result in what anyone would recognize as potent on-the-job capability development.

I've worked with other sales teams and despite the regular talk about team leaders coaching their team members to become improved sales people, the truth is it rarely happens as intended. Instead it is subsumed under the administration of sales targets, activity planning, task monitoring and firefighting.

So my first plea to those wanting to develop informal learning in each function of an organization is provide some resources to enable it to happen. If an organization wants its people to share information, then give them some time and a mechanism to do so and then encourage, monitor and reward those that do. My earlier book *Complete Training* was really a manifesto for how training and development could and should happen in 21st-century organizations. One of the key principles was that 'What gets measured gets done'. This is nowhere more true than in actively participating in informal learning.

Sometimes the answer is obvious

Want people to coach others? Train them to do so and then monitor their coaching activities.

Want more experienced staff to share their knowledge with less experienced people? Provide a platform or mechanism for them to do so and then recognize and reward those who help others to get up to speed more quickly.

Want people to spend less time on courses? Model the alternatives and gather performance data on how successful those alternatives are.

The budget paradox

There is a concern that those engaged in L&D have failed to adapt to changed times. Some of those changes have been as a result of the financial crisis and the changed nature of commerce in the years since the 2008 crash. In many cases this has led to organizations that are not merely slimmed down but positively anorexic, struggling to continue to deliver similar outputs with fewer people and fewer resources. Other changes have been a result of technological change. Still others have been as a result of a changed demographic in the workplace. In the first quarter of the 21st century it will become increasingly common for there to be four generations working alongside each other.

Capita Learning and Development – the UK training arm of the global consulting group – surveyed business leaders of 100 of the largest 500 UK firms in 2010 and found a serious disquiet amongst those business leaders.[1] In his report John Harris of Capita described how 70 per cent of business leaders feel staff skills shortages are a significant threat to their ability to capitalize on any economic upturn; 40 per cent believe that current employee skills are at risk of becoming obsolete and almost half feel that their company's current L&D department does not have the ability to deliver the training required to address these risks and challenges.

Perhaps most worryingly, only 18 per cent of the executives who responded to Capita's survey believe that the L&D function is completely aligned with business strategy. It is clear from the Capita report that there is a belief that training matters but that the training currently offered is neither the right training nor being done in the most appropriate way.

Other surveys and research also reflects a certain 'business as usual' mentality when it comes to developing the capability of the workforce. The amount of money spent on training, worldwide, is variously estimated to be in the region of $300–$310 billion annually.[2] Although the market is incredibly fragmented and what organizations include within their training spend varies enormously, the Association for Talent Development (ATD, formerly the American Society for Training and Development) estimated in November 2014 that on average individual employees in the US received 31.5 training hours in the preceding year, slightly increased from 2013.[3] What's more 7 out of 10 of these training hours, or roughly 21.5 hours per worker, involved an instructor in the classroom. In other words each employee receives around three to three and a half days' training per year. By and large, the remaining 30 per cent comprises eLearning modules.

This contrasts somewhat with the opinions of learners outlined in research undertaken by Towards Maturity. Towards Maturity is a UK based non-profit, community interest company that has been benchmarking the use of learning technologies in organizations across the world for more than a decade. In their April 2014 Learner Voice study, they asked 2,000 private sector employees which tools and approaches were most useful in helping them learn what they needed to do their job. Classroom courses were identified as being essential or very useful in only 64 per cent of cases – slightly fewer than two thirds of respondents. The classroom came fifth in order of preference in contrast to collaboration with other team members (88 per cent), general conversations and meetings with others (83 per cent) and Google searches and support from line managers (both 70 per cent).[4] Despite this kind of data about employees' preference for informal training approaches, organizations' L&D spend still seems focused on providing the most traditional of formal training; putting people in a classroom with an instructor.

Although there are voices throughout the world of learning and development expressing the belief that courses have run their race, L&D teams are primarily focused on designing, delivering and enrolling their people on those courses. In the Towards Maturity Benchmark study in 2014, Laura Overton, TM's managing director said: 'The "course" is no longer enough to help staff keep pace with change. The whole approach to supporting learning in the organization needs to be modernized.'[5]

Of course, not all L&D budgets are paying for conference rooms, projectors and trainers. According to Towards Maturity research, about 29 per cent of all formal learning is e-enabled.[6] This figure rises significantly for compliance subjects such as health and safety, legislation or regulatory matters. In these topics there is a much higher proportion of eLearning being used in order to enable an organization to create a record that someone has been trained and, usually, successfully passed an end of module test.

Despite the desire expressed by Overton and many others for a more flexible, informal approach to developing staff capability, there is still strong evidence of a reliance on formal training activities. This is particularly the case in management and leadership development. Good Practice, the Corporate eLearning Consortium, the Charities Learning Consortium, Reed Learning and INL Consultancy work in partnership to produce an annual UK Learning Trends Index. In 2014,[7] this report asked how organizations address what they describe as the five top management and leadership challenges. These challenges included having difficult conversations, managing performance, developing team members, motivation and managing change.

Once again, the survey found that L&D teams had a strong orientation to providing formal training courses. These top manager challenges are primarily addressed in the organizations surveyed by organizing formal, internal training courses in more than 70 per cent of cases. As the authors of the survey note: 'Despite this strong reliance upon training courses, research tells us that formal training is not always the most effective approach to meeting learning needs.'

This may shed some light on why managers seem to think developing their people is someone else's job. The UK Learning Trends Index clearly defined one of the five top management challenges as developing people (along with managing change and motivation). If managers are taken out of their workplace to learn how to develop people, manage change and motivate them, wouldn't most managers conclude that the organization really expects these issues to be dealt with via formal courses? Marshall McLuhan famously said: 'The medium is the message.' If the medium we use to develop managers is a formal training course, guess what message they infer from that.

The role of the subject matter expert

One of the reasons for using formal methods that are not fit for purpose may be the role of subject matter experts (SMEs) within the learning design process. SMEs rarely have a training or learning background and therefore have a limited understanding of the options that may be available for disseminating their knowledge to those who need it. If their experience of developing their own skills is limited to course attendance, then unsurprisingly they anticipate that their important subject should also warrant the expense and formality of a day in a hotel meeting room.

The other challenge is that SMEs can be a little obsessive about their particular subject. Every learning designer will tell you tales about how an SME wants apparently arcane information included because 'everybody needs to know everything' about their pet project. What's more, there is no acknowledgement of learning fade. In their book *Training Ain't Performance*, Harold D Stolovitch and Erica J Keeps outlined how the relevant performance of course participants actually drops after training.[8] This is because most courses explain that what was being done before is no longer appropriate but fail to do enough to build the skills and knowledge to adequately replace the previous practice. The trainee is left knowing what they shouldn't be doing but not feeling sufficiently confident to try new approaches.

Furthermore, people forget what was included on courses pretty quickly unless they have been given the opportunity to put into practice the skills and knowledge included in the classroom. In many courses designed with or by SMEs there is a 'spray and pray' approach to delivery. As much content as can be included in the allotted time is included, with little regard to the amount that will be: a) of immediate use to those in attendance; or b) remembered after a few days.

We know that cramming information into someone's head is a pretty poor way of anyone learning anything much. Anyone who cares about outcomes, rather than inputs, must resist the temptation to simply tell people as much as possible. The only way of realistically aligning learning with a need to change/enhance performance is to locate the learning as closely to the work as possible. This doesn't mean an exclusively on-the-job, informal approach, but it does mean that there needs to be a dialogue between formal input and informal reinforcement.

We can summarize the main difficulties of the over reliance on formal interventions by organizations. They include:

- timing – either the training need is identified many months before a course can be organized or the course is organized on a just in case basis and a significant amount of time elapses before the learner has a chance to apply what they have covered;
- a lack of managerial support back in the real world environment; and
- a mismatch between the skills required and the course objectives.

Notes

1 Harris, J (2010) *Learning to Change*, Capita Learning and Development, London.

2 Harwood, D (2014) How big is the training market? *Training Industry*, 6 June 2014, available at http://www.trainingindustry.com/blog/blog-entries/how-big-is-the-training-market.aspx [accessed 1 June 2015].

3 Miller, L (2014) 2014 state of the industry report: spending on employee training remains a priority, *TD Magazine*, 8 November 2014, Association for Talent Development (ATD), available at https://www.td.org/Publications/Magazines/TD/TD-Archive/2014/11/2014-State-of-the-Industry-Report-Spending-on-Employee-Training-Remains-a-Priority [accessed 2 June 2015].

4 Overton, L (2014) Learner Voice, *Towards Maturity*, 9 April 2014, available at www.towardsmaturity.org/learnervoice1 [accessed 29 May 2015].

5 Overton, L and Dixon, G (2014) *Modernising Learning: Delivering Results, Towards Maturity Benchmark Report*, Towards Maturity CIC 2014, London.

6 Overton and Dixon (2014).

7 UK Learning Trends report (2014) Survey 7 (April), Good Practice, available at http://www.goodpractice.com/learning-trends-report-2014-2/ [accessed 29 May 2015].

8 Stolovitch, H D and Keeps, E J (2004) *Training Ain't Performance*, ASTD Press (September), Alexandria, VA.

Informal doesn't mean unmanaged

5

The dilemma

While learners express a desire to learn in ways other than via the traditional course, L&D departments still primarily focus on providing training events alongside online modules managed by the learning management system. If how money is spent and how resources are deployed is any guide, there is clearly a reliance on formal approaches rather than much of an attempt to support informal learning. The area where there has been, perhaps, the most hype in the past few years, the use of social media, has had little impact. According to Towards Maturity only 14 per cent of organizations in its benchmark study encourage learners to share experiences and solve problems using online social media tools.[1]

Despite senior management disquiet about the L&D department's preparedness to deal effectively with rapid change, there are seemingly low levels of evidence that L&D teams are gearing up for new ways of working with new ways of learning.

Why does this disconnect exist? This requires the examination of two slightly different beliefs evident in the learning and development practitioners I talk to regularly.

Belief 1: Informal learning cannot be managed

As the title of this chapter is 'Informal doesn't mean unmanaged' you'll be unsurprised that I disagree with this contention. However, not all informal learning can be managed and to be clear about what may be more organized and what will always be left to a degree of serendipity, we can turn to the work of Professor Michael Eraut of the University of Sussex. Eraut's typology of informal learning (2000)[2] defines three kinds of informal learning:

1 Implicit learning: in which the learner links past episodes and events with current experiences in a relatively random fashion.

2 Reactive learning: in which the learner is reflecting on past experiences and events and checking out those reflections by asking questions, and experimentation.

3 Deliberative learning: in which the learner discusses and reviews events with others. He or she then uses the fruits of those discussions to make plans and decisions about future activities and plans to fill any skill gaps they may now have identified. The learner also rehearses how they will deal with similar issues in the future.

By creating disciplines such as project or post-implementation review sessions (PIRs) or after action reviews (AARs – an approach unfailingly used in the military) it is clear how deliberative learning can be managed and supported.

PIRs are a requirement of most project management standards (such as PRINCE2) and are specifically designed to include a 'what have we learned?' process. Unfortunately, even those projects in which the full disciplines of the project manager's craft have been deployed, the PIRs rarely adequately fulfil this role. The two other elements of PIR often take precedence. These focus on whether the project delivered on time and on budget and whether there are any improvements to the final solution created by the project. As you can imagine, getting a group of people who are specialist in an area to revisit and redesign their solution with the benefit of hindsight will open up a series of meetings that could last for a considerable time.

Questions about how well the project achieved its aims are skewed by most organizations' performance management strategies. Put bluntly, if the outcome of a PIR is going to impact my pay and/or future promotion opportunities, it's unlikely I am going to be entirely forthcoming about the shortcomings of the project. If I am to be assessed by an external project reviewer, this may result in a more objective assessment of the project's outcomes, but the first casualty of such forensic examination will be the learning of the participants. They will be more likely to regard the reviewer as judge, jury and potential career executioner than as a provider of objective insights that may fuel future learning.

After action reviews (AARs) are similar to PIRs but tend to look at specific, often unforeseen events in order to unpack them and extract the learning for the future. If the event has gone badly and there is a chance of subsequent disciplinary action, then don't expect much learning to go on. Only a very few cultures can be open and honest about abject failures. External investigators often create a similar lack of candour. Honesty is a prerequisite for the reflections that support effective, deliberative learning.

Deliberative learning requires someone to create environments in which people feel supported, not judged. These environments should enable those involved to honestly reflect on what worked, what didn't and what needs to be learned for the future. Establishing these deliberative learning environments isn't necessarily the job of L&D specialists, but if L&D teams wish to stay relevant and strategically aligned with their organizations, this might not be a bad place to start.

Situations in which individual employees may be geographically distant from others who can offer insights, or may need to discuss their experiences with those outside the organization because of the specialist nature of what they are dealing with, provide an obvious role for online communications technology. Any forum or community sharing is unlikely to happen in a public space, where concerns could be raised about matters of confidentiality, so an appropriate and dedicated platform may be required to facilitate this kind of discussion and review. This provision also creates the benefit that the material is available for others to consult thereby amplifying the benefits of the reflective process.

Reactive learning can also be supported, if not managed in quite the same way as deliberative learning. This is about the focus on culture and the role of managers in supporting learning and reflection. Employees faced with new experiences or new tasks need someone to ask the questions that emerge from their recent experiences. This is especially true of newer members of staff who will, by definition, face many more novel experiences than those who have been in the organization for some time.

> Questions such as: 'Why does this happen like this?' and 'Why do we use this process?' are useful for the organization as well as the learner. The real killer questions – 'Why don't we do it in this way?' or 'Wouldn't it be better if we did this?' – provide a seam of precious metal that most organizations leave unmined.

Think about this in relation to a new recruit. You have brought a person on board presumably because they have skills and experience you want or the potential to develop the skills and competences relevant to the role. You will, if you are a forward-thinking organization that recognizes that change is constant, have offered them a job because you think they can learn, or can bring new ideas about how things could be in the future. In these situations, a failure to both listen to these questions and answer or discuss them as appropriate is just plain stupid. Unfortunately, corporate stupidity is not especially rare.

The mechanisms for positively responding to these questions and providing spaces in which team members can try things out without fear of failure need to be created. Again, I think L&D teams have the prime responsibility to create these opportunities but they also have to build the culture and the expectation that line managers will conscientiously nurture reflection, questioning and experimentation. Team leaders and supervisors who believe that this kind of developmental activity is someone else's job should not be in the role of supervising others.

Implicit learning is a natural learning activity that all humans do without really thinking about it. This makes it difficult to actively manage and support. The best that can be done is to remind people why they have been given certain roles or tasks and point out, should it be necessary, that they have experiences upon which they can draw.

On occasions the management tasks associated with implicit learning are about removing the linkages between previous experiences and current events. In dealing with change, a process of 'unlearning' can be necessary. If new approaches and new ways of thinking, working and behaving are required, then the memories gained from implicit learning in the past can be focused on a paradigm that no longer exists. Continuously pointing out how things have changed, how new approaches, procedures and processes are required, can at least alert people to the traps of relying on 'how we've always done things'.

Belief 2: Informal learning is difficult to measure

It's quite easy to see that this would be an issue given the rather hostile environment that many L&D practitioners would seem to work in. After all, the measurement of all learning is often put in the 'too difficult' box and organizations are still extremely reliant on keeping records of how many people in how many training rooms rather than whether it made any difference to what people do. Where people capability is concerned, the great failure of most L&D teams has been to remain wedded to measuring inputs rather than outputs.

That's why informal learning is over-looked by most L&D teams. If I only ever report about how many online courses have been completed, how many training days have been attended, and the proportion of people who are compliant with whatever industry standard I must adhere to, what incentive exists for me to measure informal activity?

Of course, some firms have adapted their head count statistics to the world of social media. So the number of posts, number of tweets, number of comments and likes are assiduously tallied up as though this makes a difference. This trend has been further extended by the recent craze of gamification, where so-called social learning platforms have borrowed approaches used by commercial sites such as Trip Advisor to enable people to earn 'star learner' badges or a ranking as 'collaborator extraordinaire'. Without some kind of measure of quality this is pretty meaningless. If I can earn the same badges for posting 'Gee, thanks for a great post' or 'Terrific idea', or simply by clicking on a like button, then the process effectively rewards spam.

The like button is a particular bugbear of mine as we shall see in Chapter 7. The habit of ranking comments from individuals on the basis of the number of 'likes' garnered is a particularly effective way of shutting down debate and imposing a kind of groupthink – the condition by which the conformity with group norms overtakes individual propensity to have independent thoughts. If I am rewarded because people like what I say, then I am actively discouraged from saying anything controversial. But sometimes, considering the unthinkable, criticizing the status quo and being robust in a statement of views is the very essence of learning. We must be resistant to the practice of according importance to things that can be easily measured and be smart about how we measure the things that are really important.

Of course, the things that are really important are what people do and how well they do it. Any L&D measurement that is divorced from the measures of good practice in place across the operation is pretty meaningless. That's not to say that we only need look at our bottom line or customer satisfaction scores. Other departments will claim those outcomes so we need to examine some performance indicators of effectiveness in informal learning.

The three things I would want everyone to measure are:

1 **Manager ratings on 360 degree appraisals.** These should specifically ask team members, anonymously, how well their manager engages in their learning in their role and supports the aspirations to develop into other roles.

2 **PIRs and AARs.** Are PIRs and AARs in place and are they honest with a clear section on lessons learned?

3 **PDPs.** Does every member of a team have a personal development plan in place and does it have activities on that plan that are jointly the responsibility of the team member and his or her line manager? For example, a team member may lack confidence in making presentations. One answer might be 'let's send them on a presentation skills course'. However, how much more interesting to include a real task that matters to the line manager and the team and ask the team member who requires development to play a significant role in the presentation? The team leader and other colleagues can support the individual by organizing rehearsals, providing feedback, asking the team member to watch other presentations and note behaviours he or she would like to emulate, etc. If you have a team in which someone's PDP simply says: attend course X and complete eLearning module Y – send it back to be redone.

Above all, we must move completely away from the idea that developing people is an add-on or optional extra for line managers. If I am a production manager, no one would say ensuring production and quality targets are met should be something undertaken on an ad hoc or occasional basis. If I am a sales manager, people would be amazed if there was no way of monitoring performance against sales targets. If I run an accident and emergency department, there would be consternation if no one was managing the effectiveness and timeliness of providing care to those who arrive for treatment. But as a people manager? In this role, managing and developing people – our organization's most important resource – is a job taken on only when time allows. When it's not done, most employers have no visibility of this omission.

CASE STUDY LV=

Jason Pitfield doesn't look like a revolutionary. With his light grey suit, open-necked shirt and neat haircut he appears the epitome of the corporate manager. But what he and his team is involved with at mutual insurance company LV= is little short of revolutionary.

Formerly Liverpool Victoria and formed in 1843, LV= is now the UK's largest friendly society and has almost 6,000 employees. It provides more than five million members and customers with insurance and related products. LV= has a goal of being the country's best loved insurer. Its guiding principles are:

- Offering great value;
- Being easy to do business with; and
- Having a caring approach.

These guiding principles are communicated constantly and consistently across the company's 17 offices across the UK. Echoing the company's green heart-shaped logo, the goal and its principles are sloganized to: Sharp with a Heart.

The company hasn't always been in the best shape and over the last decade required a major reorganization to regain profitability. On the journey back to financial health over recent years LV= has also grown in staff numbers. From a low point of 900 staff it now employs almost 6,000, many of them having joined the company in the last two or three years.

Jason Pitfield joined LV= in that period of rapid growth and now holds the role of operational change and development manager. His background in IT and organizational development tells when he talks about his passion for making things work and his lack of interest in how we have always done things.

'It's really about systems thinking,' he told me after I'd spent a morning in conversation with his colleagues talking about what they have done to ensure new staff are compliant with financial services regulations and are able to be involved in the continued delivery of everything that Sharp with a Heart stands for. 'We looked at the data that showed us that we were training people for weeks at a time about things they rarely if ever used. By the time they got into the teams, they were overloaded with information and only recalled a tiny proportion. Not only that but increasing the team so rapidly – in one office by 50 per cent in just 12 weeks – meant that we simply didn't have the trainers or the training rooms to rely on a 90–95 per cent face-to-face course delivery format. We had to do something different.'

Jason told me that initially both trainers and subject matter experts were resistant to the changes he wanted to initiate. His focus was on data. As a regulated business, just about everything a member of staff does is recorded or logged somewhere and this generates data about the types of customer interactions people are engaged in; the number of calls, their duration and the number of times specific customers need to ring back to have their issues resolved. Using this data to shape the training was the start point of reducing the reliance on the training room and creating a continuous and more informal approach to learning vital skills and knowledge.

Speaking to one of the end users of Jason's revolutionary approach to getting new people up to speed and keeping them there, it became apparent there was widespread support for this scientific and rational approach. Nicola Rathbone is the manager of the first notification of loss (FNoL) team. These are the people who answer the phone when you have been involved in a car accident or your home has been flooded. They are dealing with customers at a time of maximum stress. When I met her, Nicola's computer screen was alive with real time data streams telling her the frequency and duration of calls and the utilization of staff resources.

Nicola explained her experience of the revised, systems-thinking approach to training: 'We changed the system that the team use to handle calls and of course that needed a training input to make sure everyone knew about the changes and their practical implications. We did need a training input about what the changes were and the rationale for their introduction, but this was limited to short classroom sessions. Then it was back on the floor to embed what had been taught.' The support back in the workplace was provided by claims specialists, the department that uses the information provided by the first notification of loss team. They work alongside the FNoL teams and provide detailed specific coaching about the information to capture, the customer information that should be given and the different conditions depending on the insurance product. FNoL team leaders complement this specialist input with step by step process coaching. This helps the teams balance potentially competing priorities. Claims handling are looking to reduce costs but how can this be done when the mission is to be Britain's best loved insurer? The First Notification of Loss team are at the sharp end of Sharp with a Heart.

'That's why the FNoL team leaders are involved. They support the process that is all about our principles of being easy to do business with and offering a caring service.' This is not a static process as Nicola went on to explain: 'Every two weeks we have a virtual conference spotting any changes in the process coaching requirements. This may amend the upfront training received by call handlers. It may also request a change in the process. The fact that everyone can be involved in identifying a better way of working is a real motivation.'

In all there are 106 people in FNoL across two sites. They handle 20,000 claims per month and more than 30,000 individual phone calls. 'The whole system change has worked across multiple measures. We used to average 2 calls per claim, now it's down to 1.2 calls per claim. Our customer satisfaction ratings have risen from 89 per cent in June 2014 to 92 per cent in January 2015.'

Nicola gave me a clear understanding of the scale and volume of the work when she told me about the budget for call handling. 'We have a budget call handling time. If it increases by one minute per call, I need 15 extra people – a cost of at least £300,000 per year.'

But as Rodney Assock, operational services director, told me, this is not used as a target for staff. 'We know that demonstrable behavioural analysis of what people do and how they act leads to us identifying the right ways of achieving good outcomes for our customers. We measure outcomes rather than focus on individual data points.'

In many people's understanding of life in contact centres, the pressure is all about those micro-measures of performance – time to answer, time on call, numbers of calls per day etc. 'Data about average call numbers and average call times and the ratio of different call types, these are all about planning. The planning has to be about the numbers so we have enough staff to meet our customers' expectations. But for customer facing staff, the only question that matters is "what was the outcome?"'

Rodney explained that trainers have become change agents in the organization. Their role is to convert the insights gathered from detailed analysis of the call data to understand what good looks like. The training focuses on the minimum level of information required to provide opportunity to practise and the main focus is on embedding.

'Each team has buddies and trainers to support until people have reached operational competence,' Rodney explained. 'We're embracing 70:20:10 but building from the formal into on the job. When we speak to team leader's they recognize that it is no longer just training's fault if their person is not working effectively. They have a role to play too.'

The focus is supported by monitoring of call quality. (You know that message you get when you first ring a financial services organization that your call may be recorded for training and quality purposes? Well that's what happens to it.) In some companies you can imagine that there would be a focus on policing the calls, naming and shaming those who are struggling. But in LV= the informal learning journey is reinforced by identifying and sharing positive calls and giving people models to follow and imitate.

The role of team leaders in coaching and supporting the development of their team members wasn't left to chance either. Sarah Booth is a training consultant in the business who pioneered the Belov=d programme. 'This was based on an analysis of new starter experiences and looked at what happened to people who achieved competence quickly and with the minimum of stress.' The resulting programme provided team leaders with coaching skills. This 'course' involved a half day programme explaining what the aim was and why, followed by a relentless focus on on-the-job coaching, one to ones and regular briefing sessions.

Sarah explained that, 'The key was "take one thing and make a difference". We found that successful coaches of new starters concentrated on one area at a time and then worked on that before moving on to the next thing. We also used "Wow" calls. These are monitored calls where the person on the phone really nailed it. We give these to team leaders to use in team meetings. We found everyone could identify what not to do. But people really benefited from understanding what a really good call looked like and felt like.'

Operational services director, Rodney Assock concurred: 'Our people need proxy information to help measure call effectiveness. That might be as much about coming off the call huffing and puffing as the details of what you said and how you said it.'

As well as new staff and new systems giving a more informal approach, LV= have created platforms to enable staff to ask questions and share good practice. Kim Ewin-Hill is responsible for the Innovate platform – an idea-sharing and generation tool. This online collaboration space is in its early days of development. 'Contributors can suggest anything. One of the earliest successes was a customer service representative who wanted to track their hours by logging on to the HR systems from home. An app is now in development to enable that to happen.' This focus on issues that don't make a huge difference to customers is a process of growing and learning, explained Kim. 'After the initial launch of the platform we were mostly dealing with things about HR issues, but some real innovation emerged relatively quickly. We wanted to make sure we didn't just get comments like "Great idea!" and then nothing happened,' Kim told me. To overcome this, the executive team are involved in reviewing all suggestions and ideas are categorized in five areas:

- needs work;
- considering;
- in progress;
- implemented; and
- already exists.

'This last category became a big area of learning. We found people didn't know about some of the things that already existed and by flagging them up, people found out about tools and processes they may have overlooked, never heard of or simply forgotten about.'

To accelerate the move from open ended suggestions to addressing corporate and strategic issues, the Innovate platform also contains a 'challenges' area. This is where senior staff share issues that they don't have an answer to and ask for suggestions. Jason Pitfeld is clear that this is the direction of travel for Innovate. 'We'll always have an area of the platform for any idea from any source, but our real focus will be involving people in addressing strategically important problem areas.'

The Innovate platform has benefited from Resolv=, a Q&A site that enables staff to post questions and receive answers. 'Anyone can ask a question and anyone can supply an answer,' Tash Govier told me as she walked me through the system. There are a group of 'Resolv= Pros' who review all questions and answers and do so in 24 hours. 'They were originally all subject matter experts but as people have had their answers endorsed they have earned the right to become Resolv= Pros whatever their role,' she continued.

The system clearly works. A platform built inside two days for £20,000 dealt with 2,000 questions in its first three months' pilot stage. As a result, working practice breaches are down by three per team and Tash confidently estimates the savings as around £500,000 – a return on investment of 250 per cent!

As well as being a development tool that has helped the team identify knowledgeable folks, it is also a route to releasing performance support tools and mini-eLearning modules. Lee Beck and Hannah McQueen make up the internal eLearning production team. Hannah is a graphic designer and Lee was a classroom trainer. Lee explained: 'For example, when we changed to Windows 7, we created a series of mini-eLearning modules to guide people through the changes. It was released via Resolv= in response to questions we received.'

These programmes are not tracked through the in-house learning management system. As Lee and Hannah explained 'It's important for courses around compliance and regulations that we know who has done what. But for things like these mini modules, it's all about 'how do we achieve the desired outcome'. Simply writing an explanation was going to be less help than creating a demonstration of how the software actually works.'

Team leaders are acknowledged throughout as being crucial in this journey from 90–95 per cent reliance on the classroom to a more organic and just-in-time approach to delivering knowledge and skills. Mike Turnbull and Jemma Green are involved in operational training. Their role has changed quite considerably, as they explained: 'Every month we have a release of new information based on changes or improvements to how we do things for the FNoL team. These are rolled out using 30-minute sessions in online virtual classrooms. The important thing is we don't run them. Teams of team leaders are in control of the virtual classroom sessions.'

Every training course organized by the trainers is supported by coaching sessions. A ratio of three or four team members per coach provides a coaching follow up to each training session of around three to four hours. This coaching team includes SMEs, one team leader and one trainer. As the person ultimately responsible for all training and learning activities, Rodney Assock confirmed, the focus is on achieving outcomes.

Each person also has real time data to check out their performance. Senior Operational Analyst, Al Smith, has designed a dashboard that provides centralized data everyone can use. 'This is really useful for buddies in the team. They can talk about real performance issues and identify what good looks like with the people they work with.'

Throughout this systems-thinking approach to developing a more efficient means of learning and building capability, data has been at the heart of the process. Jason explained: 'When we initially started we had a procedure called Marmalade. It became a poster-child for what we were trying to achieve. This was a compliance process we included on our training courses but no one could tell me what it did or why we trained people to use it. No one I spoke to had ever used it. So we simply cut it out of the programmes.'

It wasn't the only edit Jason and his team made. In all, the content of the sales and service training programme was reduced by 25 per cent. In claims, where the

FIGURE 5.1 The LV= learning redesign cycle

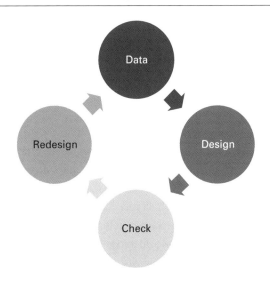

majority of new recruits are experienced staff transferring from other parts of the business, 75 per cent was removed. Jason explained that there was some resistance from subject matter experts, the executive team and trainers themselves.

'But we made the changes, produced the data and were given the greenlight to try the next thing' he told me. 'The development process was iterative for each component – whether classroom or on-the-job or performance support.' The circle he drew for me showed a simple four-stage process, and is shown in Figure 5.1.

At the end of my time in the Bournemouth offices of LV= I was impressed by a group of people single-mindedly pulling in the same direction. The use of data to reinforce their move away from the classroom had made a believer of everyone I had met.

I thanked Jason for his hospitality and for giving me access to his team: 'No problem,' he said. 'It's good to get people to reflect on the journey we've been on.'

Good – and revolutionary.

The checklist

To manage informal learning a few things do need to be in place. HR or L&D teams seeking to address some of the negative perceptions of them from the reports cited earlier would do well to focus on these things:

- **Role clarity.** The most important impact on whether informal learning takes place in a way that can be supported by the organization is the role of the line manager and other experts or buddies in a team. Everyone should be absolutely clear about the role they play and the need for them to support informal learning. As LV= found team leaders can no longer lay the blame for team member failings at someone else's door. This clarity about what my role includes needs to extend to every member of every team. Being a worker in an organization should include a demand by that organization that employees reflect on what they do and are constantly planning at least one thing they want to get better at. How do you make this work? Brief your senior team. The only question any senior team member should ask of anyone they share a table with in a canteen or get into the lift with is: 'What's your current capability improvement goal?'

- **Recognition of those who share their expertise and help others.** Whether via an online platform, such as Resolv=, or simply working alongside someone and helping them out, this should be recognized and celebrated in team meetings, newsletters and company award ceremonies. If your compensation arrangements include bonuses, it should be recognized there as well. I would argue to the exclusion of all other bonused behaviours, but let's not get carried away!

- **Recognition of those who ask questions and try to improve.** This needs to have some real thought if it is going to be more than a condescending pat on the head. If you don't have a tool like LV='s Resolv= to gather data about the questions and questioners there are alternatives. In performance appraisals, ask people to nominate the person they work with who makes the greatest effort to learn most and then interview those who get the most mentions. It goes without saying that every performance appraisal questionnaire completed by every employee however long they have been in post should include a review question asking them to describe what they have learned through their work this year and what they hope to learn next year. Writing a title of a course in this box on the form is punishable by being moved to the desk nearest the toilets.

- **Team recognition for line managers who have seen the most improved performance in their team over the year.** Those teams who have relied most heavily on formal training programmes may gain other rewards and recognition, but not this one. If you have the kind of data that LV= are able to generate, then so much the better, but every organization gathers some kind of performance data. Use what you have.

So much of this chapter about organizing and managing informal learning has rested on twin pillars. The first is thinking about the outcome required and focusing on the right solution to deliver the outcome. It won't always be about a group training session with a trainer and a PowerPoint slide deck.

The second is that the culture is pretty crucial. If the culture supports learning and continuous development it will happen. If it doesn't, no amount of imploring line managers to play their part will have much impact. But culture can have an impact, not only on how people learn but what they learn as well. That's where we are heading next.

Notes

1 Overton, L and Dixon, G (2014) *Towards Maturity Benchmark – Modernising Learning: Delivering Results*, London.

2 Eraut, M (2004) Informal learning in the workplace, *Studies in Continuing Education*, **26** (2) (July), pp 247–73.

Informal learning and culture

6

There are organizations that claim to have a 'learning culture' although what this means seems to differ. This is not to be dismissive of the claims, but they are easy enough to make and when there is no clear definition about what a learning culture actually is, then challenging the veracity of such claims is pretty hard. It is a little like non-specific organizational boasts such as 'world-class' or 'leading'. Without a set of definitions to work to, vainglorious organizations will continue to entice new recruits to their doors through the promise of a learning culture.

The claims to a learning culture is not the same as building a 'learning organization', the term coined by Peter Senge in his 1990 work, *The Fifth Discipline*.[1] This has a clear definition as an organization in which:

1 People work within a shared vision – a deep understanding of the organization's mission and values;

2 The organization applies systems thinking and recognizes that functions are interdependent and must work together;

3 There is a focus on personal mastery, an individual commitment to identifying the really important things workers need to do and setting about learning how to do them as well as they can;

4 Teams learn together, accumulating team understanding and knowledge that is stored and made available to everyone. Effectively this is the elimination of the weakest link; and

5 Applying mental models – unlearning and adapting existing values in order to develop shared values.

I'm a big fan of Senge's work but I fear that many organizations which claim that they are a learning organization have never really understood the detail of the concepts about which he writes. Among organizations that claim to be a learning organization in Senge's terms, I have seen companies in which:

- Silo thinking predominates and individual departments compete with each other. This is often encouraged by executives who have a neoliberal enthusiasm for strength through competition.

- Individuals who believe that their importance is solely measured in relation to status and pay rather than their personal capability.

- Team members who are reluctant to share what they know with others, usually out of a misguided sense of internal competitive advantage.

- Values that differ significantly between different departments, different teams within departments and between individuals in teams.

- Most damagingly, I have certainly come across organizations claiming to be learning organizations that do not have anything close to a shared vision of where the business is headed and what its purpose is, even among the handful of people making up the board or senior leadership team.

This is one of the problems of the current reliance on learning that is bite-sized and easily accessible. Senge was the founding chair of the Society of Organizational Learning at the Massachusetts Institute of Technology (MIT). His work on learning organizations is highly nuanced, based on significant research and years of observation. However, his work (and others who preach a similar gospel such as Jim Collins and Jerry Porras) has been reduced to a few soundbites. From insight to over-simplified cliché is a short journey in the modern organization.

In HR terms, organizations like to brand themselves in order to attract talent. The rise of the employer brand has seen marketing style approaches to recruitment. Attracting the best graduates along with luring good staff away from other organizations is a high priority for the modern HR director. This can't only be an exercise in vacuous re-branding. Those organizations who are serious about both attracting and retaining staff have realized that it is not enough to promise a lot pre-recruitment, but it is important to live up to the promise thereafter.

This is where Senge's Fifth Discipline is a difficult set of processes and behaviours for organizations to engage with. In the typically silo'd organizational culture, learning is seen as the job of the HR department, whereas issues of mission and vision are matters for the board. It is rare that there is someone in the role of Chief Learning Officer and even rarer for that person to be operating at board level. In some organizations the HR Director isn't a board level appointment and even if he or she is given a seat at the board, they are often regarded as a junior member of the executive team. Traditionally structured organizations that make great play of people being their most important asset, their employer brand being fully aligned with corporate values and being a learning organization with a culture of continuous learning, often assign strategic responsibility for these vital activities to someone who doesn't have a seat in the boardroom. Employing organizations that look like this cannot, it seems to me, lay any credible claim to being a learning organization or even possessing a learning culture.

How important is culture to informal learning?

Despite concerns about what a learning culture actually is, it turns out it might not make much of a difference to whether people learn informally. The presence or otherwise of a learning culture (however that manifests itself) seems unimportant in regards to whether individuals take control of their own learning and performance improvement.

This may seem paradoxical. However, in a study by Berg and Chyung there was no correlation shown between the degree to which a learning culture existed and the amount of informal learning that was happening.[2] It should be noted however that this study looked at the opinions of a number of learning and performance professionals and having asked them to define their learning culture, went on to enquire about the informal learning habits of those same learning and performance improvement professionals. There was no attempt to discover the degree to which this group were representative of the total workforce in the organizations surveyed.

However, despite my misgiving about the subject group chosen for the research, I find their conclusion interesting and credible. When they found no correlation between the learning culture (or the degree to which the organization could credibly be described as a learning organization) and the incidence of informal learning among those surveyed, they wrote: 'This may be viewed as a surprising finding, as it would seem logical that an organization with a strong learning culture would be structured in a way that creates opportunities for informal learning to a greater degree than those organizations that lack such culture. However, this may suggest that informal learning is not inhibited by a lack of learning organization structure. If a worker needs to obtain specific information to complete a task, one might assume that the individual will find a way to learn that information regardless of whether the organization has a structure in place to make that effort easier.'[3]

I have seen many management cultures where people have the role clarity I described in Chapter 5. This is a management culture that holds people to account. The tasks to be achieved are clearly expressed. This extends to what people should do, how much, how well and by when it should be completed. Ideally, the organization should set up mechanisms for monitoring achievement and allow people the space and resources to get on and complete the tasks assigned. Where this happens, regardless of whether the organization lays claim to possession of 'a learning culture' individuals will find out ways to do things. Ideally they will do so in a timely fashion and well enough to meet the requirements that they have been employed to fulfil.

Can an informal learning culture be defined?

In Chapter 2, I outlined the three components that can support the building of a learning culture:

1 Standards;
2 Structures; and
3 Collaborative groups.

The standards relate to individual roles but also to people management issues such as role profiles, PDPs and learning goals. The structures include team members who have coaching or buddying responsibilities that is recognized in both reward systems and staff planning. Team meetings should encourage consensual problem-solving and transparency. Successes and failures should be shared equally and both should be subject to blame free analysis. The question: 'How could we do things better?' should be at the heart of all project or activity reviews, regardless of outcome. Finally, collaborative groups, across disciplines and levels within the organization should provide opportunities for people to know and interact with as wide a range of people as possible. Silo thinking and focusing on the troubles of one department at the expense of an understanding of the wider enterprise supresses learning.

Some of this culture is determined by the actions of senior management – across each function. It cannot be imposed by the HR team nor manufactured without senior management support. If the CEO and the board aren't on board with this then it won't happen.

More localized culture

Of course, if you are working in a large organization that doesn't necessarily embrace these activities, then it is easy to think that you have no impact on culture, but in truth we all can and do. Those organizations that have embraced learning as the principal route to high performance, will find standards, structures and groups work most effectively, but every team can take some of these ideas and use them.

This local culture might be about your corner of the office, your team or your building. To see just what is possible if a small group actively seeks to change the culture of an organization, it might be instructive to look at examples that are negative rather than positive.

Growing a more local, team-based culture

You'll have heard it on the news in relation to an organization that has been involved in some scandal or other. These scandals are wide ranging. The behaviour of some banks in the run up to the 2008 financial crash was described as a cultural problem. The supermarkets that wield their purchasing power to the detriment of small suppliers have questions asked about their culture. Police services, hospitals and local government departments have all been condemned as having an undesirable, not to say, toxic culture. In each of these cases, senior managers professed not to know what was going on and the public pronouncements of the organization seemed to differ greatly from the behaviour of some individual employees or local teams.

If we are to believe the senior managers when they claim that they genuinely didn't know what was going on and that they certainly didn't endorse the culture that had been allowed to develop, then we can also draw the conclusion that culture doesn't have to come from the top. If these 'rogue' teams could develop a culture independent of the organization and that promoted bad practice, couldn't a positive learning culture be nurtured without top down support?

I believe it could and that each individual can either demand clarity about their role or set their own performance standards and present these to their line manager. I believe each individual and each team leader can create structures around themselves that enable them to explain things to new staff and help their co-workers improve their performance. I see no reason that individuals cannot collaborate with others in the organization to work smarter and to solve problems, even if this means snatching opportunities to meet during lunchtimes or simply creating a small area for a group of like-minded souls on the corporate intranet.

That said, I don't see examples of it happening all that often without some kind of organizational support from a middle manager or above. This might be where the L&D team has an impact, and it may also be where external consultants can have a significant role to play. In both cases, business partners can sometimes be the catalyst for reshaping the culture that surrounds a project or a training programme.

Informal learning and the dominant culture

There is a slightly more troubling relationship between how people behave and how people learn to do their jobs. If we agree that people learn informally at work whatever is happening, then the natural corollary of this is that in certain organizations and cultures, what they learn about is the way things get done around here. This is the usual shorthand definition for organizational culture once managers and consultants try not to sound too high brow. It is also the definition used by people who don't really understand the complexities of organizational culture and like to simplify culture to the level of homily.

If the first thing that a new entrant into a team learns is 'how we do things around here' then what they are learning is how not to rock the boat, how to fit in, how to do things the way everyone else does. In other words, they learn to perpetuate the existing culture.

In many instances this cultural adjustment is more formally accomplished. Induction or on-boarding programmes will talk about culture, values and organization heritage. There will be a focus on what we do and how, within any information sent out before joining or even before the applicant secures the job. Initial training and buddies will reinforce 'the way we **should** do things around here'.

In these cases, the level of transparency about the introductory curriculum means that what is communicated to new recruits, the way they are taught about the job and their responsibilities in the role, is pretty positive. Informal learning is limited to observe, imitate and experience for the first weeks and months. A certain degree of confidence and acceptance by others in similar roles is usually necessary before innovation and articulation becomes an option.

But there are organizations where induction is limited to a statutory health and safety briefing and a fitting for any personal protective equipment. Along with being informed about all the reasons why you can be dismissed, for some this is the limit of the induction. Even for those who have very precise initial training, it is far from unusual that local custom and practice so deviates from the official line that what happens once the newly inducted are placed in role is that they receive a shock about how the real world differs from what they have been told to expect. In some cases there is an attitude of pride about how different the actual work undertaken is from the expectations created during initial training. If the expressed belief in the field is that head office and the HR team in charge of induction are out of touch or that the people processes and rules don't really apply then maverick and often 'macho' management principles hold sway. My concern is not so much how people entering these environments learn, but what they learn and from whom.

Informal learning is highly prevalent in these environments. Very often, in order to survive, the new team member must learn to take the shortcuts that his or her colleagues routinely take. On occasions, some arcane rule set only properly understood by those who have worked in the organization for a long time is the governing framework. In some organizations that I have worked in, this is about protecting **us** – the workers – against **them** – the managers. The lack of trust between managed and managers can be so great that the lessons of initial training are quickly forgotten in favour of a shop-floor siege mentality.

This may appear like an old-fashioned factory style operation I am outlining and I have seen some of these activities still existing in traditional industries where industrial relations are so poor that employee engagement is what happens when two colleagues want to get married.

However, I have also seen these kinds of conflicts happening in organizations that didn't even exist 10 or 15 years ago. I have seen similar dysfunctional relationships in data processing teams employing staff to work as human cogs in a massive computerized system, contact centre workers, warehouses for online retailers as well as in household name retailers on the high street, pushed to increase margin in a difficult market.

I've seen the most egregious examples among sales teams where employees actively encourage each other to hide sales (the so-called 'bottom drawer' deals) so as not to over-achieve sales targets one month for fear of appearing bottom of the league table, with the attendant humiliation, the following month. In public services cut to the bone in the name of austerity and employers avoiding meeting employees' statutory rights through exploiting the loop holes of temporary or so-called zero hours contracts, this kind of us versus them culture is depressingly common.

Where this kind of culture exists in which the public face of the organization differs significantly from the reality of working practice, informal learning is a powerful tool to reinforce the dominant culture. Let's now look at one such example.

In the growing social care sector in the United Kingdom, most providers of care for older people unable to cope at home, adults with disabilities requiring round the clock assistance and children who are required to be looked after away from their families, are private sector providers. As part of the management of these service providers, the various inspectorate regimes require every member of staff to be certified as having obtained qualifications at an appropriate level. Everyone needs to have been trained.

Despite these clear, industry derived standards being in place, the sector has been rocked by a series of scandals, with a small number of staff in care facilities being imprisoned for their mistreatment of those in the residential facilities where they worked.

Winterbourne View and other scandals

In late 2011, a whistleblower in a residential care facility for people with severe autism and other challenging learning disabilities approached the management of the home. He raised questions about the standard of care offered and the bullying behaviour of some staff towards some residents. The owners of the care home took no action and so the frustrated employee approached the BBC. A short while afterwards a new employee at the home used a hidden camera to record some of the worst ever recorded abuses of adults with learning disabilities.

The outcome of this truly shocking revelation was that the home was closed down. In all, 11 employers were subsequently convicted of abuse and criminal neglect with six of them receiving custodial sentences.[4]

The provision of social care in the UK is governed by an inspection regime conducted by the Care Quality Commission (CQC) and providers must meet rigorous standards about the care they offer and the capability of staff responsible for its provision. Like all other residential care homes for disabled adults, every member of staff needs to have completed a minimum level of training described as the Common Induction Standards. These standards are to be locally assessed and staff are to be signed off as having met the standard and to be competent to be 'left alone'; in other words to be able to work with residents and their families unsupervised.

All the staff employed at Winterbourne View had completed this induction programme and had been signed off as competent and capable. So what went wrong?

In his judgement, Judge Ford told one care worker: 'I have read the pre-sentence report in which you say you were originally shocked by the ill-treatment of residents at the hospital but that you became desensitized to it over time. You consider that you were completely out of your depth.'[5]

Clearly, there was a failure in initial training that contributed to the problems at Winterbourne View and at other care home facilities in which similar events were subsequently uncovered. Despite new standards for common induction being introduced in July 2010[6] and being in force at the time of the secret filming, workers still behaved in totally inappropriate ways. They relied on restraint as the primary means of control and interaction with residents who, as a result of their distress and discomfort, acted in more and more challenging ways. Taunting residents became a way of combating a lack of job satisfaction and a way of venting the frustration felt while undertaking long, low paid shifts with antisocial hours.

This was a shameful example of what happens when standards are not properly understood by individuals and where an informal approach to managing competence is the preferred route for training new personnel. In these cases what is learned first and foremost is the prevailing culture of the organization. An informal approach to induction of new staff relies on immersing new recruits into the culture so that 'the way we do things round here' becomes the defining feature of the learning undertaken. Where this is positive, healthy and focused on high performance this is an incredibly effective introduction to a new role. Where the culture is poisonous or toxic, one outcome is Winterbourne View.

After these terrible events came to public attention, a series of reports looked at how things could be reorganized and, as one would expect, the role of workforce development played its role in the recommendations. As a result of the Department of Health review into Winterbourne View, a programme of action, called a concordat, was put in place. The signatories to the concordat include 50 separate organizations, many involved in workforce development and training. They included the British Institute for Learning and Development, the two main sector skills bodies – Skills for Care and Skills for Health – and a number of Royal Colleges for professional staff. The concordat committed these bodies to 'work to continue to improve the skills and capabilities of the workforce across the sector through access to appropriate training and support.'[7]

However, although standards may have changed and the vocational qualifications used in the sector were reviewed and revised, the main focus of training and development of new employees working with this most vulnerable group was informal. In their Guidance for Employers, published in February 2013, the Sector Skills body, Skills for Care, included the following advice to organizations that employ residential care workers: 'Many organizations make use of experienced staff that are familiar with and use person-centred approaches to support newer members that are undergoing induction, or who are in their first role working with people who challenge. Training itself may be useful alongside mentoring/buddying schemes and the specific art of coaching, but using in-house resources may provide an innovative, effective, and immediate solution to ensuring readiness of teams.'[8]

The in-house resources, buddying and mentoring described in this passage is a clear invitation for employers in the sector to embrace informal learning methodologies. This will lead to the culture of the employing organization being perpetuated through the means of this lower cost and more flexible mode of training delivery.

In the absence of externally defined standards of what good looks like, or where the standards are perceived to be in conflict with affordable day-to-day practice, internal cultural norms take over. When described as 'the way we do things around here', organizational culture is an expression of shared values, experiences and the way the organization treats people – whether employees, customers or service users. It is learned – often informally. Where staff feel under pressure, are under rewarded, unappreciated or not supported, then the lack of a set of clearly articulated or understood standards leaves a vacuum filled by 'the way we do things around here.' Through the scandals that have repeatedly beset this sector, some of those cultural norms have been shown to be less than positive. If the way we do things around here is criminal, that is what people learn to do and eventually become accustomed to witnessing or – in the worst example – participating in.

It would be a brave person who could read these recommendations to use informal approaches to manage induction and who would then predict that the appalling events at Winterbourne View could never be repeated.

Other scandals and the learned culture of the organization

The care sector is not the only environment in which reinforcing a toxic organizational culture has been shown to be a powerful and less than positive outcome of informal learning. Take the Hillsborough disaster. This was the 1989 English FA Cup semi-final during which 96 Liverpool football fans lost their life due in part to failings of the police operation on the day of the match. In his 2015 testimony to the Hillsborough inquests, the supervising officer on the day, David Duckenfield, reported that there was a culture in the force of learning on the job. He said: 'It didn't cross my mind to say, I'm not up to the job, I just got on with it.'[9]

What former Chief Superintendent Duckenfield had learned 'on the job' included a knee-jerk response to cover up what had really happened. He has subsequently apologised for not telling the whole truth about his authorization of the opening of a gate that led to the fatal crush of fans in the stadium. The feature of the aftermath that caused most distress to the survivors and the bereaved was that this apology and his evidence came **26 years after the event**. The culture surrounding the events of 15 April 1989 submerged the facts – and the apology due to victims – under a blanket of denial and misinformation. Such exercises in suppressing the truth are rarely the work of one individual. They are the products of a culture learned informally through the work and shared and reinforced through observation and imitation. It is hard to conclude anything other than that there was a learned culture in the South Yorkshire police force of denying responsibility when things went wrong.

Philip Zimbardo, the US social psychologist most famous for his involvement in the Stanford prison experiment in 1971, was called as an expert witness in the trials of soldiers involved in the abuse of Iraqi prisoners in Abu Ghraib Prison in 2003. In his TED Talk of 2008, Zimbardo said that social psychologists should be looking not at the individuals alone – the bad apples – but 'What are the external facts around the individual – the bad barrel?'[10] Zimbardo goes on to explore where the power lies and what the system does which makes the bad barrel. His contention is that the power relationships create the environment in which bad things happen. But it doesn't do this formally, but informally. The environment of poor initial training, a lack of clearly espoused values and pressure to achieve targets that can only be met through the cutting of corners has a powerful impact on the way in which work happens. 'The way we do things around here' could be excellent, or it could be criminal.

In these instances, those not steeped in the organization culture can have a positive effect. Zimbardo believes that perpetuating the existing group norms and cultural behaviours is not an automatic response. Individuals who come into organizations are more likely to blow the whistle, as in Abu Ghraib and in the case of Winterbourne View. Positive induction with new, well informed people coming into an existing culture may be the most powerful tool for change.

Where the organizational culture diverges from the standards that are supposed to govern workplace performance, it is difficult not to draw the conclusion that culture most often wins out. Organizational culture is reinforced by informal, on-the-job learning – whether a positive culture exists or whether it is one that is much more questionable or even reprehensible.

Is better initial training the answer?

Initial training often concentrates on the basic standards. These can be defined by vocational qualifications, or industry practice such as the common induction standards used by the care sector. The focus tends to be on those entering a particular workplace. By definition, this group are working and learning in advance of on-the-job experience. Their working practice is informed by relatively little exposure to the actual work. The training, is therefore, slightly unreal. Lacking any anchors in day-to-day practice and pressures, it can be hard to remember the detail of what has been covered. It is too simple for the initial induction to be reduced to a tick in the box.

Where there is a disconnect between the initial training course and the lived experience of the workplace, the initial training will lose out. It would be amazing if the half remembered facts and figures presented with varying degrees of skills would lodge in the mind as significantly as being immersed in eight-hour days of actually doing the job. A content heavy sheep dip is no match for experience.

Combatting culture

In an interview in 2013, Jay Cross, social learning enthusiast and informal learning guru was asked specifically about the idea that informal learning can lead to the wrong execution of tasks.

His answer is revealing: 'This can happen anywhere in life! Formal learning most certainly can result in negative learning outcomes. The main difference between these two forms of learning is that informal learning is self-correcting. The learned knowledge or skill is applied immediately and therefore feedback of whether the learning outcome has been positive, eg being able to execute a certain task, is received immediately. This immediacy is not available with formal learning as it is usually done in advance that results in learning outcomes being forgotten by the time the gained knowledge or learned skills needs to be applied.'[11]

I think this rather misses the point about just what is learned informally and formally and how they can both lead to undesirable outcomes. Cross's answer seems to be 'at least informal learning is better than formal training'. I don't think this is good enough. The approach I would advocate is to work positively with culture and align formal and informal approaches rather than reducing it to 'yah boo, informal is best'.

The four steps I would advocate organizations seeking to prepare people for a new role are:

1 Train the receiving team, especially the team leader and senior team members. Do this training in their job by working alongside them. Understand the role to be filled by asking the team how the initial training can help prepare someone for the role they need to play. Design/adjust the initial training depending on the role and the requirement expressed by the team member.

2 Involve the team member who will be undertaking the buddying or onboarding support in the formal induction session. Not necessarily for all of it, but at least ask them to come along and have a coffee with their new colleague. Ideally, get them to run part of the session.

3 Intersperse formal training with on-the-job experience and observe some of that on-the-job onboarding. Have a short period of induction followed by a period in the department in which the individual will be working. Bring them back into the classroom to reflect on what they have seen and undertake the next formal training. Finish the formal training session by creating a detailed plan about the next period of on-the-job learning.

4 Review the learning with each new starter and their buddy/team leader at regular intervals until the end of the employee's probation period. At each review (one month, three months and six months is a minimum frequency) discuss what learning needs to be addressed on the job and set clear targets for what good looks like. Role clarity is an essential to support people in undertaking focused informal learning – especially in the early days of the job.

Sounds time consuming and expensive? In early 2014, Oxford Economics conducted a survey that concluded that the cost of replacing an existing employee was on average £30,614.[12] Not inducting people properly is reckoned to be a significant reason for both high absenteeism rates and high staff turnover in many organizations.[13]

But the real lesson from looking at culture is that informal learning will generally reinforce and perpetuate the existing culture of the organization in which employees work. Working alongside people and collaborating with colleagues to resolve issues and learn new skills is rarely able to tackle truly dysfunctional working cultures. Where these exist, informal learning can only be a supporting part of the solution. Change management processes including formal measures are the only approaches worth thinking about in response to the scandalous cultures outlined here and elsewhere. There are some cultural problems for which only formal training will do.

One of the major cultural changes organizations have had to face in recent times revolves around the use of technology. Specifically organizations have had to reflect on how people will interact in a connected and networked role. As so much informal learning is facilitated via information and communications technology, surely in this regard informal learning is the route to creating the culture we all need to work in. I'm not so sure and in Section Two, I'll investigate the role of technology supporting and occasionally hindering informal learning at work.

Notes

1 Senge, P (2006) *The Fifth Discipline: The art and practice of the learning organization*, 2nd edn, Random House, London.

2 Berg, S A and Chyung, S Y (2008) Factors that influence informal learning in the workplace, *Journal of Workplace Learning*, 20 (4), pp 229–44.

3 Berg and Chyung (2008), p 9.

4 Hill, A (2012) Winterbourne View care home staff jailed for abusing residents, guardian.com, 26 October 2012, available at http://www.theguardian.com/society/2012/oct/26/winterbourne-view-care-staff-jailed [accessed 19 May 2015].

5 Hill (2012).

6 Common Induction Standards (2010) Guidance for those responsible for workers in an induction period, Skills For Care (July).

7 Department of Health (2012) Winterbourne View Review: Concordat, programme of action (December), Department of Health, London.

8 Skills for Care/NDTI (2013) Supporting staff working with people who challenge services, Guidance for Employers, Skills for Care (February), Leeds/Bath.

9 Barlow, E (2015) David Duckenfield admits responsibility for deficiencies, *Liverpool Echo*, 10 March 2015, available at http://www.liverpoolecho.co.uk/news/liverpool-news/david-duckenfield-admits-responsibility-deficiencies-8813776 [accessed 29 March 2015].

10 Zimbardo, P (2008) The psychology of evil, TED talks, available at http://www.ted.com/talks/philip_zimbardo_on_the_psychology_of_evil?language=en#t-508577 [accessed 29 March 2015].

11 Webanywhere (2013) Informal learning vs formal learning in businesses – interview with Jay Cross, webanywhere.org, 25 July 2013, available at http://www.webanywhere.org/blog/informal-learning-vs-formal-learning-in-businesses-interview-with-jay-cross/ [accessed 2 June 2015].

12 HR Review (2014) It costs over £30K to replace a staff member, report of research undertaken by Oxford Economics, *HR Review*, 25 February 2014, available at http://www.hrreview.co.uk/hr-news/recruitment/it-costs-over-30k-to-replace-a-staff-member/50677 [accessed 2 June 2015].

13 See ACAS advice for details about the link between poor staff training and induction and attendance and staff turnover issues, ww.acas.org.uk.

SECTION TWO
Liking ain't learning: the rise of social and the impact of technology

It would be churlish not to accept that Web 2.0, the so-called 'read–write' web, has not had an impact on our ability to learn informally. Being constantly connected to information via the World Wide Web has changed the world of work for pretty much all of us. Not only are we connected to data, news and information, we are also connected to people. Conversations with colleagues, competitors, consultants and conspiracy theorists are only a click away.

In this section I'm going to explore how technology has impacted our ability to learn informally. In some cases it has smoothed the path to skills and knowledge and widened horizons. In other situations it has been less of a boon than some may believe.

Liking, learning and looking up the answers

7

I received a phone call the other day. It was my daughter – her smartphone had been playing up and she was in the provisions aisle of a supermarket on her old and under-whelming handset – you know, the ones you can do things like ring people up on. Anyway, she was in a minor turmoil. Planning a recipe she needed to know how to convert millilitres into grams. 'I haven't got Google on this!' she said, plaintively.

I understood her plight. We have become so used to accessing instant facts on our smartphones, tablets and PCs that we find ourselves unable to recall basic information from schooldays – or at least unwilling to trust our memories on these things. Looking things up has never been easier and will never be the same again. As computers become wearable and our internet access becomes permanent, only a social and cultural rejection of being always connected will change our 24/7 internet-dependent lives. Whether this is a good thing or a bad thing, whether a cultural revolution that will reject the ubiquity of Facebook, Google, YouTube and Twitter will start anytime soon, I leave you to be the judge.

The World Wide Web and the many sites, apps and platforms that rely on it seems to me to have been, on balance, positive. There is nothing wrong with having an unimaginably thorough encyclopaedia at all of our fingertips (or wherever the next generation of devices will be located). Giving each and every one of us the capability to publish our thoughts, opinions and theories and to share the nuggets we find with friends and family is also OK. However, as the Huffington Post reported in July 2014: 'You may have been surprised to learn that Facebook experimented on nearly 700,000 Facebook users for one week in the summer of 2012. The site manipulated their news feeds to prioritize positive or negative content, attempting to determine if emotions spread contagiously through social networks. There was no age restriction on the data, meaning it may have involved users under 18.'[1] These and other recent exposés about the lack of privacy that entails and the business models of some of the 'free' platforms that we use to publish pictures of our break-fast/cat/toddler may give some of us pause for thought. The whole idea of a web that no longer restricts our roles to those of consumer but now enables each of us to be a writer, film maker, photographer or artist seems generally positive. That said, I could live without the cute videos of kittens in boxes but I guess every advance has its price. Those same platforms that open up the world of publishing, sharing and collaboration are being increasingly touted as learning tools and in this regard I'm not so sure.

The rise of the Mavens

The growth of the enthusiasm for the use of social media tools in learning (if not its actual practical use in this regard) is exponential. This enthusiasm is primarily brokered by what Malcolm Gladwell in his seminal work of 2000, *The Tipping Point*, called the **Mavens**. Gladwell described the Mavens thus: 'To be a Maven is to be a teacher. But it is also, more emphatically to be a student. Mavens are really information brokers, sharing and trading what they know.'[2] The world of training has more than its fair share of Mavens. The fragmented nature of the industry leads to a high proportion of those working in it being sole traders and/or part of loose affiliations of contractors and small businesses. Many of the businesses that have employees and offices – as opposed to a space on a kitchen table during term time – share a commonality with the self-employed trainer in that often they are built around the ideas, brain-power and presence of only one or two individuals.

This group of trainers and business consultants has always had a stock in trade of performing as a Maven. Inspired by a desire to establish 'thought-leadership' or simply publicizing their work more brazenly, it is they who have populated the conference platforms, the industry magazines and the network meetings. By definition, the leaders of businesses engaged in running courses are good value at conferences. Articulate and unfazed by standing in front of an audience, they are natural speakers who are used to being listened to with rapt attention. In the field of publishing, the initial forays onto the internet relied heavily on begging and borrowing articles from these Mavens. In a world that hadn't quite worked out how to monetize their web presence, a raft of small scale online publishers started websites aimed at the workplace training market, and drew their content from the donated articles provided by those thought leaders in charge of training departments and running small scale training companies. These were paid for via an extra line on the CV and a link to the company's website.

Once the opportunity to be published arose without the slog of having to persuade a website owner to take an article it is unsurprising that this group became avid self-published bloggers and, latterly, tweeters. It is not uncommon – nor particularly surprising – for the early adopters of a technology to be powerful advocates for its utility. And so it is in the training field among our Mavens. They have embraced social media and see possibilities only imagined in the unenlightened times of a world governed by more formal publishing. For a group who are mostly characterized by a fairly uncompromising stance in relation to commerce and the world of capitalist endeavour, it is ironic how quickly our Mavens have taken hold of the means of production. Marx would be proud.

Now before you run away with the idea that I am sneering at these Mavens, the self-appointed thought leaders of the business training industry, I must point out, dear reader, that I am one of them.

For the past 20 something years I have been speaking at conferences – almost always unpaid – I have donated articles and, once the opportunity presented itself, I have blogged with the best of them. I, too, am an early adopter of social media – active on twitter with a regularly updated LinkedIn profile and a Facebook page linked to my website. This is not a polemic by a sneering outsider.

As the Mavens – me included – have outlined their thoughts about training and development and how organizations can improve their practice in developing their workforce, it was inevitable that the medium would become the message. The debate, which is what it quickly became albeit one in which everyone seemed to be pretty much on the same side, soon turned to the use of social media as a tool to support learning and development – especially among knowledge workers like the Mavens themselves.

I'm a bit anti social

This caused the first issue. What do we call this new phenomena? Training is old hat and implies someone with knowledge and skills imparting them to someone who should have them now, or in the future, whether they think they need them or not. The buzzword used to describe what we all do, by those of us engaged in improving the capability of employees, has been development. But social development sounds like we're operating a finishing school before launching our graduates on polite society. This wouldn't do at all.

The other focus for training people has been learning. I used to do a cheap gag at conferences: 'What's the difference between a training officer and learning officer? About five grand a year – boom, boom!' But despite my cynicism that often what is described as 'learning' is actually just training in a more expensive suit, the terminology has stuck. So what do we call learning that uses social media? Why, of course, social learning! Except …

Social learning is a term that is already taken. If you consult any psychology book – especially about child development – you will find the name of Albert Bandura, the most often cited living psychologist. He came up with his 'social learning theory' in the 1960s by looking at how children imitated what their peers and – crucially – important role models did through observation.[3] Subsequent studies have observed how chimpanzees, whales and other mammals learn novel ways to forage or new techniques to hunt by imitating the behaviours of skilled members of the troupe, group or pod.

This does not seem to me to be what is happening online in social networks. Whether employees have access to a publicly available social network such as Facebook or Twitter or whether there is a purpose built tool on the corporate intranet, the process is not imitative. It is information sharing. When in the hands of our Mavens it is also mostly a way of information sharing with few of those consuming the output doing much beyond reading it and moving on to the next thing.

Now some have attempted to justify the use of the term by citing Bandura. One Maven of the old school recently penned an article in which Bandura's focus on social interaction was claimed to be just as valid a discussion of what happens on twitter as it was as a route to explaining how a group of three-year-olds in the 1960s imitated the adult behaviours they had observed. The role model/authority figure in these interactions is central to social learning theory, the presence of what Lev Vygotsky called **a more knowledgeable other**.[4] In Vygotsky's social development theory, the more knowledgeable other (or MKO) is usually thought of as being a teacher, but in practice could be anyone who knows more about, or is more experienced in the particular area where learning is required. The person who determines whether a person is an MKO is the learner. The attempt to hitch the social media wagon to these well researched child development studies seems to be a strained relationship at best. In fact, the whole idea of a community in which we are all teachers and yet no one is, seems central to the basic premise of the use of social media in the learning sphere. My reading of social learning theory seems to completely dismiss such a free-for-all. The teacher/role model/MKO is an essential component. The social learning nomenclature just won't do. It is opportunistic, inaccurate and lazy. Most disappointingly for those who are allegedly at the forefront of innovation, it is unimaginative.

Perhaps if the old Mavens who had a track record and business services or a book to sell (a position of self-interest that at least keeps them relatively honest about what they say in the public domain) were the only figures generating content in this new world, then social learning theory might – just might – be germane. But they have been joined by a whole new group of contributors. The ease of access to the new world of user generated content sharing means that anyone can post whatever they want, and seemingly they do. The information may be of variable quality, un- or at least under-researched and lacking references or evidence to a degree that would shame a first-year undergraduate student. But the power and ubiquity of the always on web is such that whatever is published is taken as gospel truth by some who access it. As learners, it seems we crave the teacher's authority and are prepared to invest it in others pretty indiscriminately.

So we have a dilemma. Information is being shared in a new democratized environment. Despite the apparent democracy, most of what is published and available is created by the people who always had routes to have their opinions and their theories accessible to those who were interested – the Mavens. The web was always a route to making existing activities more convenient; to enable them to be conducted more quickly and the output available more widely. If we compare self-publishing in the training sphere with other forms of web commerce – for example selling goods direct to consumers – we can see a similar pattern. For the most part, the organizations that have been successful pre-web continue to be successful post-web having changed their business processes and their routes to market to accommodate this new channel. So it is with training and development. The established Mavens have a more convenient, quicker route to market that is even more accessible to a wider audience than traditional alternatives. The breakthrough innovation of the web has simply amplified the existing voices.

What inroads that have been made to these platforms and channels by the previously voiceless can lack authority. Although for a few of those who have found a voice through new technologies I'm not convinced that they would not have been able to find a route to get their words and ideas out there without the option of user-generated content. What's more – and this is almost blasphemous among some of the most militant adopters of social media in learning and development – maybe their output would have been improved had there been some element of editorial control, requiring citations, evidence and references.

Learning or just copying?

The world of social media in learning and development is far from rosy on one other essential component. Is the exchange of information characterized by the tweets of our Mavens – and the authority-light blogs of any new sages who have joined the Mavens' ranks – really learning?

In the spring and summer of 2013, a group of researchers overseen by Iyad Rahwan worked with 100 subjects at the University of Oregon. The object of the experiment was to see what difference a social network made to the ability of learners to perform analytical tasks. The results were clear. The cognitive reasoning tests have been used in many different experiments and are accepted to be effective measures of the ability of an individual to overcome their initial, intuitive response to a question. For example, one of the questions asks:

A bat and ball costs $1.10.
If the bat costs $1 more than the ball, how much does the ball cost?

The intuitive response to this question is 10c. However, if that was the answer, the bat would cost $1 and therefore be only 90c more expensive than the ball. It requires a degree of analysis to work out that the true cost of the ball is 5c, the bat $1.05 and therefore the total cost $1.10 with the bat costing one dollar more than the ball.

One group simply answered the questions – alone and unconnected to anyone else. They became the baseline group. Thereafter, groups were asked the questions individually and then given access to the answers of others in a range of different networks. In one network, each person was connected to just five other people. In another, everyone was connected to everyone else and there were other varieties of network, including one that replicated the well-connected position of our Mavens – that is, the people with the most connections found it easier to make brand new connections and therefore had an increase in access to user answers to enable them to compare and draw their conclusions.

Having seen the answers given by others, everyone could change their answer and on the second go, generally people were more likely to get the answer right than on their own. Social learning appears to work.

But on subsequent questions designed to check a similar kind of analytical thinking, the answers prior to seeing the responses of others were no better than those of the baseline group. This was true regardless of the nature of the network in which the user was involved. In essence, while performance had improved in respect of the immediate task, through copying the answers of someone else, the ability to work and think independently and to avoid the self-same instinctive traps in subsequent, similar questions remained unchanged. As the authors of the study noted: 'This observation suggests that there are limits to the efficacy of social learning in propagating successful reasoning strategies. As "cultural learning can increase average fitness only if it increases the ability of the population to create adaptive information",[5] our results exemplify imitation as a form of free riding that ultimately may not improve society's capacity to innovate through analytical reasoning.'[6]

Now this seems to me to be at the heart of the debate about online learning generally and using collaboration across networks in particular. Those of us with children will recall our toddler's first foray into the spoken word. As two- and three-years-olds demand parental attention with phrases like: 'Look, Daddy, Look Mummy. I jump.' We may correct their sentence construction. 'It should be: "I am jumping",' we gently advise. Some days later, perhaps at the local swimming pool our child demands our attention again. 'Look Daddy, I am swimming,' they call.

This is the eureka moment in language development. From the particular, that is the grammatically correct 'I am jumping', the child has figured out the general – the construction of a similar sentence in a different context using a different verb. This is learning. If Rahwan's experiment were to be translated into three-year-olds mastering their mother tongue, they would have corrected themselves about 'I am jumping', but by the time they got to the pool they would be demanding our focus with: 'Look, look I swim!'

Remember in Chapter 2 I defined learning as **acquiring new or modifying existing knowledge, behaviours, skills, values, or preferences**. I would question whether copying someone else's answer (as seen in the Rahwan experiments) can be characterized as learning in the context of this definition. In part – acquiring knowledge – maybe, but what knowledge is to be acquired? Is it the answer, or the route to finding the answer next time? As the ancient proverb has it: 'Give a man a fish and you feed him for a day; teach a man to fish and you feed him for a lifetime.' In cyberspace, perhaps we are more engaged in donating fish than providing courses in the basics of angling.

If we are not interested in developing the capability to work out answers because, using the constantly available internet the answer can always be checked, then we meet a new challenge. As my daughter discovered in the supermarket aisle, there are some issues with delegating our memory to a device.

The brighter side of social media

So far so gloomy. I am not, however, without hope for the use of social media and user-generated content as a route to learning. There are some opportunities to harness individuals' engagement with Web 2.0 technologies (the so-called read–write web of which social media is a significant component) to accelerate their learning. This may extend to developing the kinds of analytical skills and reflective behaviours that constitute learning beyond the particular towards a translation into the general. But it will require a much more structured approach and possibly a cultural shift if we are to harness these advantages. It is certainly more than making sure everyone knows what hashtag to look for.

It requires independent off-line thought and behaviour if we are to genuinely learn, however well and frequently we are connected. The required cultural shift may start with trusting our instincts a little more. The conversion rate for millilitres to grams is one to one. This is a relationship about metric measures taught in primary school. To break free from the safety net of Google and liberate ourselves from a reliance on copying the answers of others will be the real cultural shift in ensuring that social learning doesn't make us more stupid than we were before. As Rahwan notes in the commentary on his experiments: 'The unreflective copying bias can alone explain why increased connectivity may eventually make us stupid by making us smarter first.'[7]

Social media has its role but must be used cautiously. Increased collaboration over time and distance can deliver greater individual and collective competence. To gain the benefits without falling into the many bear traps that exist in the use of social media as an adjunct to learning and capability development will require a range of techniques and structures. What those techniques, structures and skills might be is the essence of what follows.

Notes

1 As an example, see http://www.huffingtonpost.com/2014/07/21/facebook-terms-condition_n_5551965.html.

2 Gladwell, M (2000) *The Tipping Point*, Little Brown, Boston, p 69.

3 For a primer on Albert Bandura (and other learning theorists) see: www.learning-theories.com/social-learning-theory-bandura.html.

4 Vygotsky, L S (1978) *Mind and Society: The development of higher mental processes*, Harvard University Press, Cambridge, MA.

5 Boyd R, Richerson P J and Henrich J (2011) The Cultural Niche: Why social learning is essential for human adaptation, *Proceedings of the National Academy of Sciences* (USA) 108: 10918–25.

6 Rahwan, I, Krasnoshtan, D, Shariff, A and Bonnefon, J-F (2014) Analytical reasoning task reveals limits of social learning in networks, *Interface*, Journal of the Royal Society, 11: 20131211, available at http://dx.doi.org/10.1098/rsif.2013.1211 [accessed 29 May 2015].

7 Rahwan *et al* (2014).

Is there hope beyond the social media hype?

8

I am a user of social media (or SoMe as recent trends would have it). As a small business person, a writer and a knowledge worker, social media provides marketing tools that would otherwise require an army of PR people to replicate. I have blogged – irregularly – for the last five years and I use my Twitter feed to point people towards my blogs and my presence in other online forums and to promote my books.

I also use Twitter to follow certain individuals in the training and development world. Some of these are people I respect and I read their articles, follow links where available and use this as source materials for my own writing and training practice. As a Maven, I am both teacher and student.

Beyond the L&D bubble

So why do I think the use of social media as a learning and development tool has been over-hyped? The first reason requires us to look beyond the hyperbole of the Twitter feeds of the digitally savvy Mavens and seek evidence of these Web 2.0 tools being used by people who are involved in some endeavour where training and development is not their primary role. The Chartered Institute of Personnel and Development (CIPD) undertook two surveys in 2013. The first involved over 2,000 people in employment and was undertaken by YouGov PLC, a leading opinion research and polling organization. The second survey of almost 600 people was undertaken by CIPD and designed to understand how SoMe was being used in relation to organizational policies and Human Resources (HR) practices. Reflecting the

CIPD membership, three-quarters of respondents in this second survey worked in an HR department, with communications and learning and development roles also featuring strongly. Interestingly, this second survey excluded people working as sole traders and as I said in Chapter 7, a significant proportion of the training industry in the UK is made up of one person businesses.

Of those in the first survey, over 76 per cent use social media in their personal lives. Despite almost two-thirds having a mobile digital device that they used for work (laptop, smartphone or tablet) only 26 per cent of respondents use social media for work and only 18 per cent of those surveyed felt that social media was 'important' for their work.[1]

Now, hang on a moment. One in four doesn't seem to me to be an overwhelming level of use of social media. In the slightly more recent Towards Maturity report, that I referred to in Chapter 4, as few as 14 per cent of organizations in its benchmark study encourage learners to share experiences and solve problems using online social media tools.[2] Remember, this is a benchmark study where organizations voluntarily sign up to compare how well they're doing in relation to learning and training technologies. You would expect them to be slightly ahead of the curve before taking the time to complete the benchmarking questionnaires. Yet, despite these underwhelming responses about use of social media in organizations, in a survey of the top technologies for learning and performance carried out by the Centre for Learning and Performance Technologies, the top learning tool every year between 2009 and the most recent survey in 2014 was Twitter.[3]

Why the disconnect? The CIPD report has a view: 'The relative lack of interest in using social media for work can be taken in two ways: employees have yet to understand its value, or the advocates have overestimated its value.' They go on: 'Claims made by social media advocates who predicted widespread transformation appear exaggerated.'[4]

One group who do find social media useful and are enthusiastic adopters are freelancers. I reiterate, the training and development industry in the UK and elsewhere comprises a high proportion of freelancers. The lonely worker in their home office is likely to reach out to like-minded souls across the ether. Lacking the real life social interaction gained from working in an organization, is it any surprise that this group uses Twitter and other social media platforms a lot? The problem is not that they use it – I know how isolating working alone can be – the problem is that they are apparently unable to take the perspective of others who are not in their position. They seem unable to imagine that what happens during their working day is not the same as the experience of many others working in organizations. Perhaps this projection of their own experience might account for some of the exaggerated claims that the CIPD refer to in their report.

There may be many explanations about why work-based social media usage by those employed in organizations would appear to be so low. One is that the policies and procedures that might allow the necessary freedom (on which social media depends) are simply not yet developed. Put simply, if you are an office worker and you post an opinion on a social media site that does not necessarily reflect the views of your employer, you may find yourself in a somewhat tricky position. The discourse about social media at work has been as much about people being dismissed for their Facebook status updates as about collaboration between colleagues. In the CIPD survey, 29 per cent of employers have dismissed or disciplined a member of staff as a result of their use of social media in the year preceding the survey.

Similarly, because of the word 'social' there is a natural disquiet about using publicly available platforms while at the office. In the late 1990s I designed eLearning programmes that included elements of game-play within them. They were designed to be fun and engaging while dealing with serious messages about subjects that could be described as a little dry. Rather than boring people to tears with endless references to legislation, the team I was working with and I designed – admittedly pretty basic – decision-making games to help people understand what compliance with particular legislative and regulatory requirements might actually mean. The challenge we subsequently faced was for the designated audience of these programmes to be allowed to use them. As groups gathered around computer screens and the merits of various options were discussed, my clients in the training department were assailed by complaints. 'Why are you asking people to play damned silly games?' was the cry from disgruntled line managers.

Fast forward 15 years and I don't think that the attitude of a line manager to her staff spending work time on Twitter, Facebook, LinkedIn and the like is going to be that much different. In fact, even in organizations that have social media policies in place and provide clear guidance to their staff, there is still anecdotal evidence that both managers and co-workers can be hostile to those using these platforms during the working day. Admittedly this may change over time. As the CIPD report also noted: 'Limiting misconceptions, such as that Twitter is irrelevant if you don't want to know what people have had for their breakfast, can be expected to wane.'[5] But my point is that this hasn't changed yet and as a regular Twitter user I do find people who unfortunately blur their social and professional lives to an unhelpful

FIGURE 8.1 Percentage of workers using social media for work-related tasks

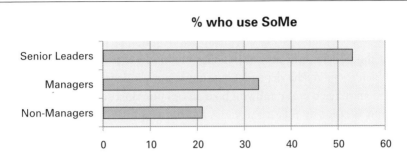

degree. Perhaps this may explain why the CIPD survey found that 59 per cent of respondents believe that their organizations restrict access to social media because of concerns over time-wasting and almost two-thirds of those who do use social media at work are using their personal smartphone or tablet rather than their employer's computer network.

There are more interesting figures from the CIPD research on who is using social media at work and why. One big surprise is that senior leaders seem to be much more active on social media at work than the people who work for them (see Figure 8.1).

With more than half of all senior leaders who responded to the survey using social media, it seems that those who already have access to the means to have their views published and discussed are once again dominating these new platforms.

So, as our senior leaders and freelance Mavens make most use of social media it would seem that there are certain events that would be great opportunities to explore how social media can provide insights and even can promote one's learning.

You had to be there

In 2012, I couldn't make it to a conference that – for many years – I had attended. As an experiment I decided to try and follow the proceedings on Twitter via the conference hashtag. It wasn't easy and one of the reasons for this difficulty was that so many of the users of the hashtag were somewhat indiscriminate in their use of it. I would follow someone who seemed to be tweeting useful stuff but subsequently it turns out they have thumbs that move faster than Usain Bolt being chased by a hungry cheetah and it is imperative that their followers must know that:

a they have had a pit stop at a service station;

b the trains are delayed; or

c if they remembered to pack an umbrella. (Usually they didn't, by the way. Over disclosure is really not necessary.)

Following an HR event via Twitter presented a certain flavour to the proceedings. So strong was this flavour that after a while it seemed that one of the UK's leading training and development conferences was actually wholly devoted to social media and, specifically, Twitter. I read across a number of tweeters in an attempt to iron out the partiality of one individual's take on a particular conference presentation. Despite widespread sampling of the tweets emanating forth, in essence, what was being said could be boiled down to: 'Look at me using Twitter.' Marshall McLuhan was right – the medium really *is* the message.[6]

After a few days, conference presentations were posted and I was directed to them via the same hashtag and some of these were useful. Being flavour of the month, social media did indeed have a significant place on the conference programme. Reading more considered reports of these presentations was interesting. But the hype couldn't be controlled for long. One report included this fantastic comment from a platform speaker: 'I recently became a mother and I used my mobile phone apps to learn "how to be a mother". I didn't ask experts, I asked other people in the same situation as me for their experiences via social media.'

So that's okay then – no health professional was involved in this process, no midwives, no doctors. No books consulted? Nothing learned from the extended apprenticeship in parenting commonly known as childhood? Really? Interestingly some days after this report was posted it was updated. This particularly hyperbolic endorsement of social media was removed. It seems even the most enthusiastic promoters of social media can tell that there is line between selling the benefits of their chosen toolset and just being plain silly.

The point that I think that speaker was trying to make was about online collaboration. Reaching out to one's peers in a network to ask questions and using the so-called wisdom of crowds to help you reach a conclusion. There is some merit in this as a concept but again it would appear to be the preserve of a few and not as mainstream as the presentations at that conference would suggest. Neither has it become business as usual which, if your number one tool for learning and development is Twitter, you might think was the case.

The premise explored by the social media evangelists is that individuals can collaborate on projects via social media tools, pick up new and smarter ways of doing things through this regular not to say 24/7 contact, and thereby learn on the job from individuals engaged in the same or similar work. Once again the CIPD research throws up some surprising statistics when investigating collaboration via social networks.

Instead of this being the primary use made of social networks at work, fewer than 4 in 10 keep in touch with people outside their organization and fewer than 3 in 10 keep in touch with people inside their organization. Remember, this is of those who use social media at work: 26 per cent of those surveyed. Thirty-eight per cent (the figure for those collaborating externally) represents fewer therefore just 9 per cent of the working population. Of those collaborating internally, the figure is only 7 per cent. To base a learning strategy on this level of collaboration would seem to be optimistic at best.

Where's the sense in seek-sense-share?

The great guru of online collaboration is Harold Jarche, a personable Canadian oft quoted and something of the Mavens' Maven. He talks about personal knowledge mastery and specifically, the **seek-sense-share** framework, which he defines thus:

> **Seeking** is finding things out and keeping up to date. Building a network of colleagues is helpful in this regard. It not only allows us to 'pull' information, but also have it 'pushed' to us by trusted sources. Good curators are valued members of knowledge networks.

> **Sensing** is how we personalize information and use it. Sensing includes reflection and putting into practice what we have learned. Often it requires experimentation, as we learn best by doing.

> **Sharing** includes exchanging resources, ideas, and experiences with our networks as well as collaborating with our colleagues.[7]

Now it may come as a surprise that I actually agree with some of Jarche's ideas here. I think in terms of developing one's knowledge, going beyond simply reading the tweet and clicking the link and liking the blog is essential. But there are two specific disconnects. The first, as the CIPD research shows, is that this isn't happening to any significant extent at work. Jarche runs courses that will help L&D teams work out how to improve this state of affairs. At a recent webinar I attended, he noted the irony that in order to learn how to do this stuff a course was needed, whereas surely 'social learning' would be enough to deliver the required knowledge and under-standing to go forth and implement a personal knowledge mastery cam-paign for your knowledge workers. When questioned, he was also disarmingly honest and explained that he hadn't worked out 'how to mon-etize his intellectual property' through using a social network to disseminate these ideas. As I mentioned earlier, the Mavens' use of social media as adver-tising or a route to market is not an insignificant factor in assessing their contributions.

The other disconnect is that if you are fortunate to attend a conference in person (as opposed to attending via Twitter), the presentations and discus-sions about social media use for learning and development fail to make these distinctions. In fact, it all seems to be very simple with hardly any effort required from learners at all. I was at a conference towards the end of 2013 – this time as a real live delegate – and I found that every learning management system or eLearning platform now came with its own 'social learning tools'. These were not the models envisaged by Jarche that would require a learner to find information out, work with it and then share their responses to their network. These were star ratings for modules and 'like' buttons – a hybrid of Facebook and amazon.com. Where these kinds of tools had been used at all, which wasn't very often, examples provided by speaker after speaker featured two kinds of 'user-generated content'. The first is a series of posts – written or increasingly using video – in which senior people give their employees the company line. The idea of user-generated content, that is real users who are peers to the learners, was seem-ingly consigned to the 'too difficult' box.

The second type of content was what I call 'online presenteeism'. This was a series of posts from the learners that were unerringly positive. They included such valuable learning insights as 'Thanks for sharing this' and 'Cool, this is really useful'. It is the equivalent of the boy in the junior school class jumping out of his chair with his arm raised whenever the teacher looks his way. It is more about being noticed, than being engaged. Attention-seeking behaviour is always slightly irritating when observed from the detached perspective of someone whose attention is not being sought.

Online presenteeism just takes up space. It is neither sensing nor sharing as defined by Jarche and certainly it is not learning. Yet the numbers of comments are proudly paraded around conference halls and smug refer-ences to the large number of active users who 'contribute to the learning content' ensure these new platforms walk away with the awards at the gala dinners.

An uncomfortable pat on the back

Now it's only right at this stage that I fess up. In 2010, I was lead designer for the programme that won the best online or distance learning programme at the eLearning Awards. The judges remarked: 'The judges admired the forward thinking blending of media types and peer-to-peer functionality in this excellent platform for marketing skills development.' Now the judges may have liked the 'peer-to-peer functionality' – that was shamelessly modelled on the ratings and reviews of Trip Advisor coupled with an 'ask the expert' forum – but the award was won after only six months of live usage. After a couple of years, the verdict would be somewhat different. The peer-to-peer functionality was a great feature but it didn't deliver the benefits that either the judges or the design team anticipated. I suspect I am not the only award winner to feel that by emphasizing the features that seem innovative or in tune with the Zeitgeist, the normal rigour of an award category – did it make a difference? – can be somewhat sidestepped. I believe that what we designed was a good programme and worthy winner, but the solid features of good eLearning design coupled with on-the-job support were much more important factors in its success than the fancy social media-style bells and whistles. Still, the gala dinner was nice.

The 'it's really great' comments existed in that programme and continue to be the mainstay of user commentary on social networks. Do they provide any value at all? They should not be characterized as endorsements that can be given any weight and they are not something that constitutes a 'push by a trusted source' to paraphrase Jarche. Surely not even the most committed who trust their child rearing skills to Facebook would categorize these interactions as any kind of curation.

But the role of the curator is interesting indeed. I agree with Jarche that the idea of having someone who recommends things to you is useful. It mirrors the role of the More Knowledgeable Other as defined by Vygotsky and which I wrote about in Chapter 7. However, in practice, once again the experience of this role is somewhat variable. I regularly read a blog by Donald Clark.[8] He is a real Maven and always interesting, stimulating – especially when he says something with which I disagree. The debates on the comments pages of his blog are worth spending time over and if he points me to something via his Twitter feed I know it will be valuable.

Other Mavens have a lower level of quality control. One regular tweeter, blogger and collaborator of Harold Jarche's, recently directed her Twitter followers, of whom there are many, to a presentation on the SlideShare platform.[9] If you don't know it, this is a platform on which anyone who signs up for a free account can publish PowerPoint and presentations in other media. The company's mission is to 'build the world's largest social content network' and it was recently acquired by LinkedIn. SlideShare is a prime example of a Web 2.0 platform.

I clicked on the link about **The Future of Work** and found a presentation of outstanding banality. It was not only infantile in its presentation (I have a bit of a thing about cartoons being used as a medium for business communications) but was factually incorrect in a number of places. In fact the number of errors was such that the whole premise of its argument (that the presence of young people in the workforce means that businesses need to change) was fatally undermined.

I replied via a tweet to the person who had alerted me to its existence, briefly outlining the errors in as much detail as 140 characters allowed. I received a very terse comment suggesting I raise this with the presentation's author. My opinion is that a 'curator', tweeting a link, bears some responsibility for the factual accuracy of the sites they recommend. This belief was clearly *not* shared.

I did as was suggested, signed up and posted a comment pointing out the error of the material. I received no reply, but I was then included in the updates for every other comment made, of which there were many. The lengthy comments were – like mine – generally pointing out an error of disagreement or an alternative point of view. These were very few indeed. The majority were of the online presenteeism variety – 'great deck – thx for sharing', 'An amazing presentation' etc, etc. In fact there were – last time I checked – 46 posts in total, mostly one line compliments. These knee-jerk affirmations would seem to be more about the individual being seen to have read the content than about any kind of engagement with the material in the way that Jarche advocates in the sensing or sharing stage of his framework. If they communicated anything at all, they all said the same thing: 'You have confirmed my prejudices'.

Far more significant – at least numerically – was the other form of online presenteeism – Likes. There were 10 times as many of these. But what put all this into context is the fact that at the time of writing, this presentation has been viewed 118,000 times! Do the maths. Less than 0.5 per cent of readers had interacted with the material in any traceable way – with likes or comments. Only 0.04 per cent of readers commented and only 0.004 per cent had commented in a way which showed a real engagement and questioning of the subject matter. If this seems to you to be less like a learning revolution and more like added noise in an environment with significant information overload, then you're not alone. In the CIPD survey, 48 per cent of those who use social media for work complained that it 'leads to information overload'.[10]

A flock of twits

I'm not sure what you call a group of people who communicate via Twitter. I've seen them described as 'Tweeps' which feels too cringe worthy to be used more than once. 'Tweeters' seems too descriptive and 'followers' plays up to the megalomania of some of the people present on the platform. For some of the behaviours I am about to describe, only '#Twits' will do as the collective noun.

I follow a relatively modest number of people in Twitter – low hundreds rather than thousands, and yet scrolling through the posts still takes a significant amount of time. I regularly reduce the people I follow – especially if I find myself passing straight past their 10, 12 or 15 posts per day, that often turn up in a single block. (If they are after publicity, why do they think this might work? If they're trying to help the 'community' – how do they think this meets anyone's needs?)

Nonetheless, managing the limited number of people I follow on Twitter takes a lot of time and energy. The energy required may be overlooked. I find it exhausting filtering the useful from the banal, the professional comment from the opinion of the latest act to appear on The Voice.[11] With so much noise, it can be an assault on the senses, like visiting a shopping mall with promotional campaigns designed by hyperactive three-year-olds. The clamouring for my attention can be wearying. To reduce the load I try to have fixed, limited times for monitoring Twitter. Without these self-imposed limits, the jumble of inputs could easily take up a very significant part of my working day. It is simply too unmediated to be of significant use and I regularly question the cost (in terms of my time) versus the occasional benefits I derive from my involvement.

Conclusion

To summarize, social media at work is far from the predicted revolution and more a small area of unrest in some pretty isolated circles. The kind of cultural and behavioural change to harness the potential of Web 2.0 tools and platforms to improve learning and capability development is some way away. There are possibilities in the ideas put forward by Jarche and others. However as it stands we are living in a world where most users knee-jerk from seek to share. Little, if anything, is sensed. The process of use, experimentation and engagement with what has been found and that according to Jarche is a requirement of his Personal Knowledge Mastery is subsumed under the need to be visible, vocal or present.

We are so far away from addressing the various barriers to enable effective engagement with online content that we must start from some fairly basic principles and try to do so in an environment that is based on experience, with some clear standards and expectations. We will only be able to do this, if we get rid of the obsession with the process and the hype about its as yet unrealized benefits.

One of those basic principles to think about is the skills needed to be an active and effective participant in social media. That's where we are headed next.

Notes

1 Gifford, J (2013) *Social technology, social business?* CIPD, London.

2 Overton, L and Dixon, G (2014) *TM Benchmark – Modernising Learning: Delivering Results*, Towards Maturity, London.

3 Hart, J (2014) 2014 Top 100 Tools for Learning, available at http://c4lpt.co. uk/top100tools/ [accessed 30 May 2015].

4 Gifford (2013), p 32.

5 Gifford (2013), p 32.

6 McLuhan, M (1994) *Understanding Media*, MIT Press, Cambridge, MA.

7 www.jarche.com.

8 donaldclarkplanb.blogspot.co.uk.

9 www.slideshare.net.

10 Gifford (2013), p 27.

11 The Voice is a UK-produced 'talent' competition featuring amateur singers covering the songs of so-called popular artists. You have now been warned. Don't blame me.

Smarter social tools?

> Two old colleagues meet each other unexpectedly. They share news and as they prepare to go their separate ways, one turns to the other and says: 'Hey, let's connect on LinkedIn.'
>
> You're on LinkedIn?' says his ex-colleague.
>
> 'Yes' he replies.
>
> 'You never said you were looking for a job.'

OK, so it's not the best joke you ever heard, but when it comes to using the different social media platforms, context is all. The chief determinant of context is what you want to get out of your involvement with social media.

Let's assume you have signed up for a social media platform, or enrolled onto an enterprise collaboration platform – such as Yammer – because your primary rationale is that you want to learn. You may also have a secondary requirement. Perhaps you wish to promote yourself within, or external to, your organization; or to promote your organization and its products or services. The way you use social media platforms and the skills required will slightly differ depending on the hierarchy of these wants.

In the CIPD's *Social technology, social business?* report, the researchers found a number of reasons for using social media at work:

'Engaging with social media is about being part of something larger than ourselves. It is not primarily a medium we use to broadcast and promote ourselves. It is inherently beneficial, of value in and of its own right, more than it is instrumental to financial gain. Discussions and press coverage of social media often refer to boastful or crass comments, inane sharing of details of our personal lives and postings of "selfies" (photos taken of oneself on a mobile device), but it seems that our use of social media is less narcissistic and more collaborative than we are often given credit for.'[1]

The report's authors commented on these statistics which show reported usage as follows:

FIGURE 9.1 How people use social media at work; from CIPD report

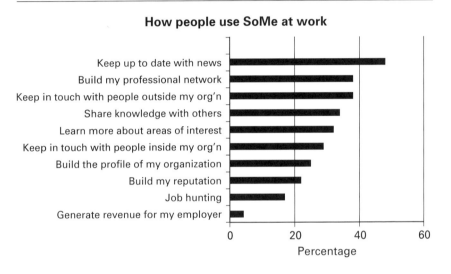

I think this assessment of what is going on with social media fundamentally misses out one significant factor. Social media is a performative space. The projection of our personalities on social media is not necessarily who we are, but the person whom we want others to see. We are selecting our image and wearing the costume which most accurately fits the sense of self we wish to communicate to others. (This performativity extends to the personalities we display when answering questions about how we use social media in self-reported studies, but that is another discussion altogether.) The authors of the report were prepared to view the respondents' desire to share knowledge with others as a sign of altruism and that building our professional network is not 'broadcasting or promoting oneself'. This seems an unusual interpretation of why people spend time on their LinkedIn presence. The fact that 'build my reputation' did not figure more highly in the survey's results wasn't because people have rejected using social media as a route to enhancing their own profile and importance. It is that they have realized that 'performing' as though their reason for spending time on Twitter, Instagram and LinkedIn is to big themselves up only serves to build a profile as a shameless self-promoter. Social media users prefer a little more subtlety than 'Look at me, I'm dead good, I am!'

The performative nature of social media provides interesting indicators of culture. If people think that sharing knowledge or being generous with their expertise is culturally approved, it will gain them kudos. From kudos comes recognition as a thought leader and from thence comes improved career opportunities. The question for organizations is how can they harness this desire to be seen as a 'good' person when enlisting people to engage in sharing their knowledge?

If part of an individual's rationale for using the available platforms is marketing – either of themselves or of their organization, its brands, product and services – then there is plenty of guidance available for the use of social media as a route to building a profile. Some of the advice about engaging widely and building connections may run contrary to the learning requirement. It is one of the areas where volume and value compete. In traditional, commercial social media – ie using these tools for self- or brand-promotion – volume is all. The more followers you have the better. One way of getting more followers, unless you are already famous or infamous, is to connect to, follow or friend more people. Whichever social media platform we're discussing, those who are best connected find it easier to make new connections. If, however, the reason for using a social media platform is to further one's own knowledge and understanding, a degree of pickiness is required. The intelligent learner using social media seeks to connect with those who demonstrate at least some of the characteristics of the role models that he or she would choose in a non-digital space.

Beware the crowd

However, the commercial interests of the social media platform providers demand that we are slightly less discerning in those that we hook up with in cyberspace. Most social media users have too many connections, friends or followers to have a meaningful digital relationship with any of them. Where online connections are an extension of a real, face-to-face relationships, there may be additional levels of opportunity to learn, share and discuss, but for the most part, the average user is simply overwhelmed by the thought leaders, Mavens and direct marketers to win out in the time:benefit analysis stakes.

If an individual does seek out the myriad followers which their self-esteem (or lack thereof) demands, managing the potential information overload and background noise creates an ever-decreasing return on the time invested in scanning, monitoring, retweeting, liking and commenting on their posts. This may be especially true when the focus of one's social network is an army of contacts who agree with your world view or position on a specific topic. I attended a webinar recently – as it happens, about the use of social networks in learning. What was evident from the 'backchannel' (that is: the text-based conversations which go on between participants, commenting on the input from the presenter and posing questions) was that there were a substantial number of people on the webinar who knew each other quite well. Whether these were virtual or actual friendships is not altogether clear, but from the tone of the conversation, I would hazard a guess that most of these people knew each other in the realm of meet-ware rather than software.[2]

As we awaited the webinar's commencement, there were many *waves* between chums across the backchannel. Perplexingly, many of them continued well into the session – like naughty schoolchildren chatting at the back of the class. The chair of the webinar joined in and, seemingly encouraged the conversation in the backchannel while the presentation progressed. This may have been to elicit contributions and questions but these attempts never moved beyond 'nice to see you' pleasantries. It seems for some, social is more important than learning.

The atmosphere created was less one of inquisitive studiousness and more like a club. I had stumbled into a virtual room inhabited by mates chatting about something they all knew and agreed about. This was a conversation of the converted. The best indication of this was that after only three minutes the presenters were thanked for running such a great session. We'd only got to the agenda by this time. Whatever followed wasn't going to detract from the assessment. This was great – regardless of what, if any, insights were to be shared.

The limitations of algorithms

There is a world of difference between the wisdom of crowds and the ignorance of the mob. The 21st-century internet, focused on advertising revenues and targeted messages to part you from your hard-earned cash, has become reliant on building a profile of your internet use. Information is then served up to you based on your interests, linking your previous online activity to sites and online experiences which share similar characteristics. Sometimes this is done well, providing options to explore topics further or find things one wouldn't otherwise have discovered. However, the algorithms aren't always that smart. When I bought children's books online when my kids were still at junior school, the sites I used then seemed to believe that this represents a lifelong interest in fantasy novels aimed at pre-teens featuring talking animals. It doesn't.

In networks, social bookmarking aggregates knowledge. Essentially, content which has been marked important or relevant by the most people to whom you are already connected appears higher in subsequent searches. But as with online petitions and other attempts to reach out to citizen opinion via the web, these are subject to being manipulated or hijacked by those who are sufficiently well-organized to marshal their followers. When Barack Obama came to power in 2008, he established 'We, The People'[3] – a petition-based website designed to make government both transparent and accountable to the electorate. The results may have been predictable. Apparently, every single state in the USA wants to secede from the union and become independent (a total of 700,000 signatures if you add all the petitions on this subject together). There is a demand for the day after the Superbowl to become a national holiday – called National Hangover Day. Those upset by one-time talk-show host and UK national Piers Morgan advocating gun control gained significant support in their request to have him deported from the USA. Of course, the very first petition to reach the threshold of receiving a government response concerned the legalization of marijuana. This was rapidly followed by the demand that the US government acknowledge that space aliens are real and have regularly walked the Earth. The link between these two petitions has not been made. The good citizens of the USA would appear to be a little less cynical than I.

Skilled information seekers

In some ways, citizen petitions which promote views outside the mainstream are a symptom of the immaturity of online interactivity. For the LV= Innovate platform (described in Chapter 5), the initial posts were concerned with airing minor staff grievances or addressing other dissatisfactions. However, LV= are prepared to persevere with the idea. Their hope is that as the system becomes business as usual the benefits of harnessing the creativity and problem-solving skills of those doing the work will eclipse the use of the platform as a tool for discussing discontent. Other employers are less far-sighted and initial expressions of staff concerns are enough to kill information sharing and collaboration projects stone dead.

There is another concern about constant connectivity which relates to media literacy. The proliferation of the internet has provided a stage for crackpots far more dangerous than US students who want to legalize cannabis. Conspiracy theories abound on the web and the levels of misinformation provided by those with a particular axe to grind can be breathtaking. In a considered essay on the use of misinformation distributed via social media, Peter Pomerantsev describes the campaign waged by those favourable to Russia in its attitude to the replacement of the pro-Russian government in the Ukraine.[4] He tells the story of 'troll-factories' in which internet savvy Russians are employed to post pro-Russian disinformation on social media along with grotesque stories about leaders hostile to the Russian cause. He cites cases where easily disproved stories are distributed in such numbers and with such speed that although they are patently inaccurate they flood the internet to such an extent that they gain credibility. As traditional news outlets are squeezed by new media sites, they reduce their staffing levels in response to falling sales and advertising revenues. All journalists are taught to ensure balance in their reporting, but starved of fact-checking resources, that desire to tell both sides of the story inevitably includes examples of crude propaganda. As Pomerantsev notes: 'The side that tells better stories, and does so more aggressively – unencumbered by scrupulousness about their verifiability – will edge out someone trying to methodically 'prove' a fact.'

The genie is out of the bottle on the use of the internet and specifically social media as a source of information for 21st-century workers. It is a feature of our working lives which needs to be managed. When even journalists feel compelled to repeat baseless propaganda – whether about the conflict in Ukraine or about climate change or about the motivations of a former member of the boy band One Direction – then employees using similar sources to learn will need guidance on verifying what is accurate and reliable. I was recently reading an industry website in which the first four articles were promoting facets of a single viewpoint. The fact that all four authors were part of the same organization was not revealed anywhere in the accompanying text. Whether that means that what they wrote is unreliable or focused towards gaining commercial benefit does not automatically follow, but this is useful background information when judging the perspectives taken in these four pieces. Without that knowledge, the person stumbling across these pieces may believe that there is a groundswell of learned opinion driving inexorably in one direction. The obscuring of the fact that these opinions were effectively all coming from the same source served to amplify the power of their aligned messages.

Unmediated or relatively lightly mediated access to the web means that people have the freedom to express their beliefs regardless of the basis of those beliefs. With enough likes and star ratings ideas from the doubtful to the downright dodgy can gain a credence which they do not deserve. If the web can be manipulated in this way, then the potential to promote a point of view or set of beliefs using social bookmarks and other aggregation tools may present the triumph of received wisdom over fact. Despite significant research pointing out the paucity of evidence regarding such learning sacred cows as NLP and learning styles, the friends of these discredited approaches regularly ensure their high ranking in social bookmarked searches. A cynical and questioning frame of mind is essential to make sense of the un-moderated or moderately well manipulated internet.

The threat of like-mindedness

However, as organizations wishing to develop the capabilities of connected learners, the targeted information sharing reflected by social bookmarks seeks to manage the range of information available via the web. The idea of filtering the vast range of opinion which is out there makes sense. Trying to be open-minded on the web could leave time for very little else in the working day. However, this narrowing of our experience of the web's cornucopia presents a problem. Our people are potentially cut off from information which presents an alternative view, which challenges their beliefs or which makes them think. Being made to think is surely a key element of the learning experience.

In 2012 and 2013, the Open University continued its excellent contribution to the study of education and the development of practice as new technologies open up possibilities for educators. In its second publication of its series on innovating pedagogy, the writers turned their attention to what they called seamless learning – the idea of complimenting the classroom with information-seeking and data gathering facilitated by technology. They described the pros and cons of having information served up to us via the web, thus: 'This personalized "me-shaped world" is a form of seamless learning by induction: we come to see the world as constructed around our interactions with it. The benefit is that relevant information may always be ready to hand, but the danger is that this prevents us from seeing alternative perspectives. We may come to believe that our experiences, views, preferences and connections are not just the most relevant, but all there is.'[5]

What I witnessed during the webinar I described earlier was the me-shaped world in action. The wisdom of crowds and the nature of connected enquiry had been reduced to narrow groupthink. Instead of benefiting from a web, the participants had enclosed themselves in a hive.

As technology insider Andrew Keen says in his 2015 book *The Internet Is Not The Answer*: 'Just as Instagram enables us to take photos that are dishonest advertisements for ourselves, so search engines like Google provide us with links to sites tailored to confirm our mostly ill-informed views about the world.'[6]

Avoiding groupthink and the narrow, not to say superficial, engagement with a subject is one of the challenges which requires a new skillset for both learners and those supporting and facilitating the learning of others. Some people may promote the idea that personal learning is the responsibility and sole concern of the individual. Within the corporate sphere, where collective capability is a vital consideration, the process of building competence cannot be abdicated to each individual. Strategically, a business which considers its people its greatest asset – and they certainly all say that they do – needs to manage the performance and capacity of that asset. Utilizing Web 2.0 technologies effectively to achieve increased capability cannot be left to chance.

Individuals do have a responsibility for managing their own learning, within the framework established by the organization. However, as we saw in Chapter 8 and the output from the CIPD research, the current low take up of employment focused social networks would suggest that unsupported, individuals will not naturally gravitate to the available platforms. An intervention by the organization is required to encourage take up and a continual role in supporting, monitoring and curating will be required to underpin continued capability development.

How is this to happen? In the first instance we need to return to the informal learning model and see where the organization can best intervene to increase the efficiency and effectiveness of the use of technology as an aid to learning, rather than merely confusing background noise.

Learning from IT companies

To investigate how the focus on technology can work as an enabler of capability, it is perhaps sensible to turn to IT companies to see if there are models which can be applied more universally. Certainly, IT teams have long used forums and communities to ask questions and develop their skills. If you have recently purchased some new software the chances are that you were also invited to enrol on the forum which supports it. There, you will be able to access demonstrations of how to use the software, tutorials on key functionality and the opportunity to ask questions of the developers or of other users. As you become more experienced in your own use of the software, you'll be able to answer questions, especially if you've found a way of doing something which wasn't anticipated by the system's designers. Software companies create these mechanisms as an alternative process to a help desk. The typical IT help desk is a routinized process of help tickets and problem resolutions by hard-pressed techies who find themselves answering the same questions repeatedly. Creating a mechanism which reduces contact to the help desk and incorporates a more dynamic version of the frequently asked questions (FAQ) pages which proliferate on the web is a no-brainer.

Communities and forums also provide a mechanism for the development team to consult with clients on new features and the changes required to subsequent releases. Members of the forum will gain early access to beta releases of new versions of the software and be asked to review and comment on the revised version. The IT industry has long been adept at using its customers as free software testers.

It seemed to me that IT companies would be early adopters of online collaboration as a way of providing routes for customers to learn how to use their products. I was interested to understand what the challenges were which had to be overcome and the degree to which these approaches were transferrable to other skills beyond the realm of bits, bytes and broadband.

What I initially discovered, however, is that the process of educating people in how to use the technology on their desk is relatively old-fashioned and for the most part relies on courses, certification and manuals. Apart from reminders via online help functions – performance support tools at the more formal end of our continuum – there was little organized innovation in the use of collaboration and social networking as a means of learning. Where such platforms existed they tended to be genuinely informal and set up by users who wanted to share their expertise/frustration with the software their employer had adopted.

CASE STUDY SAP move to 'social learning'

In the major IT companies, one name repeatedly crops up whenever technology is discussed with major organizations. SAP provides enterprise management software to many global enterprises. Many of its clients have SAP programs acting as the spine of their operations, from managing inventory, procurement, ordering systems and HR. If you get paid on time, if your order is processed correctly, if you are able to run just-in-time manufacturing the chances are that SAP have created the technology which makes these things happen. The SAP promise is to 'help organizations fight the damaging effects of complexity'.[7]

As such a core element of many organizations' activities, it is hardly surprising that SAP has an education team designed to train end users in how to get the most from its software. Once you have programs of such ubiquity, unsurprisingly the demand for these training and education services is high. The numbers are staggering: over 500,000 individuals trained annually, 420,000 certificated SAP users, 29,000 partner training events, 3,000 partners providing training for their clients and employees, more than 600 eLearning courses and over 400 live virtual classroom sessions available in nine languages. But despite this admirable scale, there was still a challenge. Although over half a million people are trained every year, SAP realized that the potential audience was somewhere between 3–4 million people and the existing reliance on trainer led sessions and facilitated virtual classrooms was not going to be able to cope with a seven- or eight-fold increase in demand for training.

SAP are on a journey led by Arnold Jung, who is the Director of Business Transition for SAP Norge. 'Our intention was to both increase the scale of what we offered but also to maintain a dialogue with those who needed to learn how to use our products,' he told me.

The approach had other strategic aims. Rather than simply providing more training, the intention was to alter the role of SAP education, moving from an add-on source of revenue to a critical driver of software adoption. The strategy was predicated on creating greater and greater confidence with SAP products across the full product range, thus providing a barrier to companies choosing to shift to a different software platform.

The sheer scale of the potential user numbers lead Arnold's team to consider how SAP could become a catalyst for more self-service and informal learning, integrated into the workflow of its users. The really disruptive idea was to completely turn the business model on its head. Instead of charging users on a transactional basis – ie for each course, virtual classroom or certification process – initial interactions with SAP Education would be free. The SAP Community Network (SCN) is completely free to register and each registered user has a profile with information about their areas of expertise, any existing certification and, should they wish, their CV. The registration is undertaken by an individual user, rather than by their employer or the SAP client business. As a reward for signing up to the platform which bears a resemblance to other social networks like LinkedIn/Yammer or Facebook, the registered user can access expert led sessions, and a sandbox area where new content is tested.

As the registered user accesses the SCN, there are opportunities to earn points for certain activities. This use of gamification is inventive and encourages users to 'pull' content from the site as well as preview the subscription services which are available on an individual or on an enterprise basis. 'The community has now grown to around 2 million individual SAP users,' explained Arnold. 'Our aim is to encourage users to subscribe to the learning hub which is based around learning rooms and represents a much more efficient way for our facilitators and experts to interact with the community.'

There are now 60 learning rooms covering different subjects and led by SAP facilitators and moderators. Social in construction, they host a number of content pieces. Registered members of the community are periodically invited to use otherwise paid for content. If they review that learning content or post a relevant question or comment they earn points which not only makes them more visible on the SCN, it also unlocks other content free of charge. 'At the moment our focus with the learning rooms is to gain traction.' Arnold went on: 'We want to increase usage and hopefully attract those users who are prepared to collaborate, to post and join discussions. At the moment the learning rooms are still "pushing" content to users and are still actively managed by SAP experts and facilitators. Our aim is to create much more "pull" and early signs are that it is happening but it requires significant work. After all, we are changing the way people have learned about our software for many years. It is bound to take time.'

CASE STUDY Assima introduces smart
performance support

Another organization changing technology learning is Assima. Their Vimago technology is also used to support SAP installations, but can be configured to work with companies' own software and other packages. As with Arnold and his team at SAP, Tony Coates and Eleni Iatridis at Assima are desperately trying to engage people in pulling learning content to help them learn as they work.

As Tony told me: 'We found that "push" functions, when we can check what the user is doing and send information are only really useful if someone is about to do something they shouldn't.' The Vimago technology watches the learner using the software and can intervene if the individual is about to do something against policy (such as approve a purchase above a customer's credit limit) or use a piece of software which they haven't been trained to use. 'Our system has a feature called App watcher,' Tony said as he demonstrated the software at work. 'It runs in the background checking what you are doing and constantly interrogating your learning management system to ensure that you are appropriately certificated to undertake the transaction you are involved in. If you're not the system can freeze you and direct you to the relevant training. This is extremely useful if, for example, you were working in financial services and someone was about to do something which would cause problems with regulatory authorities.'

But the real interest in Vimago is not what it does which is very smart performance support, but in the way it was designed. Eleni Iatridis is Assima's Chief Learning Officer. The product development process fell to her. 'We used an evolutionary process to help develop some of the functionality in Vimago,' she told me. 'The development team had created the product with the capability but there was no clear path for how it would be used and what benefits it would bring to our customers.' Like many IT companies, Assima has project engineers and developers 'on the bench' – essentially in between projects before being deployed to the next project which requires their skillset.

'During their time on the bench, developers and programmers often update their skills or learn new software. We asked a group of them to contribute to the evolution of the product. Over a three month process we worked collaboratively with a small group drawn from various teams in Germany, the USA and the UK. By virtually meeting together every other day we were able to collaborate to create a series of demonstration objects, test them rapidly with internal teams – sales, finance and purchasing – and refine the demonstration objects so we could equip the sales team with a product they could explain to customers.'

The performance support tools needed to work with four different audiences:

1 Brand new software users, post-initial training;

2 Delta users – people who were very experienced with the software but needed to understand new functionality or new internal rules;

3 People for whom training could not be organized for whatever reason for whom performance support tools would be the only way of learning how to use the software; and

4 All users, to deal with common problems or errors.

The resulting performance support is constantly available, on multiple devices, and works primarily in 'pull' mode – in other words if the computer user needs help, the support available is highly contextual. Because the system knows what you are doing, a range of different help buttons will be available so if the user can't remember the information they need to enter into a particular box, they can ask for advice just about that area of the interface.

Tony Coates was clearly proud of the resulting package which Eleni and her team had produced. 'We focused on providing usable performance support which a user can access while they are doing something else. The people using these software packages may be on the phone to a customer at the same time, it needs to be smooth and unobtrusive.' As well as providing immediate support, the scratch for the specific itch, the system also remembers that you have asked for that support. If a user repeatedly needs help with a particular function, the tool will direct them to other content or training opportunities to address those areas where they lack confidence.

Application beyond applications?

If you've ever tried to master a new piece of software, you may have had a similar experience to me. I have attended sessions where I have been shown how to use a piece of software and given the opportunity to practise certain functions. Days, weeks or months later, when I come to use the software again, I have only the faintest recollection of how to access certain functions or the sequence I should try to do things. The trial and error which follows is frustrating and time consuming.

It seems that focusing on IT-based learning as closely as possible to the actual use of the software, is eminently sensible and somewhat overdue. If rules and functionality can be summarized into mini-scenarios or step-by-step sequences, then so much the better. Where the requirements I may have are slightly more complicated, or where I am a brand new user unaware of precisely what functionality is available, then free 'drop in' access to a series of tools and experts seems to make sense.

However, I am still unconvinced that the kinds of innovations underway at SAP and Assima can be transferred to the more nuanced world beyond IT. In software there is usually a 'right way' to do things and through collaboration and communities, perhaps alternatives and shortcuts which remain fit for purpose can be shared, discussed and modified. Beyond the world of software, however, the application of similar performance support tools may be unable to match the help offered so precisely to the context. Not only that, but software basically does what it is told to do. In the messier areas of endeavour, such as working with people, we may need an alternative to the binary right and wrong of software development.

Notes

1 Gifford, J (2013) *Social technology, social business?* CIPD, London, p 12.

2 Meet-ware, I discovered a few years ago, is what techies call people! It relates to the fact that people who are less wedded to their computer screens actually waste time getting together face to face rather than resolving all issues via forums and communities. I think this might be illuminating in relation to the interpersonal skills of some computer geeks I have encountered!

3 Available at https://petitions.whitehouse.gov/ [accessed 30 May 2015].

4 Pomerantsev, P (2015) The Kremlin's hall of mirrors, *Guardian*, 9 April 2015.

5 Sharples, M, McAndrew, P, Weller, M, Ferguson, R, FitzGerald, E, Hirst, T and Gaved, M (2013) Innovating Pedagogy 2013: Open University Innovation Report 2, The Open University, Milton Keynes, p 18.

6 Keen, A (2015) *The Internet is not the Answer*, Atlantic Books, London.

7 Available at http://go.sap.com/about.html [accessed 30 May 2015].

Social networking skills for learning and collaboration

10

One of my concerns about social media and the tools used for online collaboration is that they are being asked to do so much more than they were originally designed to accommodate. Facebook started as a platform for male geeks in US universities to meet members of the opposite sex. I'm not sure that this sort of platform is capable of adapting to collaborations that possess levels of complexity way more complicated than the mating habits of the average Harvard student.

Personal knowledge management: a daily job

Unquestionably, the amount of time spent on updating one's personal knowledge could be never ending and Jarche advocates a filtering process designed to find and keep the things that are of interest and relevance (see Chapter 8). Other writers on the topic similarly urge a regular process to cut through the noise of the internet.

Marcia Conner of Sensify has written extensively on the routes to utilizing the various networks of which a worker is part: 'Learning is constructed in situ, through conversation and circumstance, supported by relationships and trusted networks. It can be augmented with collaboration technologies that encourage people to surface experiences and content across location, operating system, and topic.'[1] Conner goes on to describe the Learning ARC – an acronym for Access, Recommend and Curate in which Access is finding things you need or are of interest, Recommend, the process of dissemination via social media tools, bookmarks and blogs and Curate, to keep a personal library of content available for subsequent reference, both for the individual finding the information and for others in his or her network.

I think there are dangers here. The seek-sense-share model advocated by Jarche and others has a crucial step of using or making sense of the unmediated content – acting to filter the information before sending it on to others. The process of doing something with the information that has been sought out seems to me to be an essential part in the learning of the individual and in the power of any subsequent recommendation. Its absence in the ARC model suggests additional noise rather than insight.

In *Rethinking Knowledge Work* published by global consultancy firm McKinsey, author Thomas H Davenport, president of information technology and management at Babson College, writes: 'Most knowledge workers haven't been trained in search or knowledge management and have an incomplete understanding of how to use data sources and analytical tools. Productivity losses can be substantial. Even before the advent of social media, workers in one 2005 survey sponsored by America Online and Salary.com cited personal Internet use as the biggest distraction at work.'[2]

Davenport goes on to say that knowledge workers are relatively unskilled at sharing knowledge and when they do it is of little use to others within their organizations. A focus on sharing available information but using, synthesizing and explaining information is at the heart of a more structured approach to learning in a network.

If we combine the informal learning model – from observe to articulate with the seek-sense-share model, we end up with a more manageable approach. This synthesis of models helps us to filter the myriad potential inputs from our internet-powered networks.

In this expanded model (Figure 10.1) we can see how networked and collaborative learning corresponds to these five stages, with the 'seeking' taking place at the point at which the learner discovers he or she needs to understand or do something new. The sensing stage – which, in Chapter 8, I contended was frequently absent – takes place through the imitation and experience stage and into the innovation stage. At the innovation stage the learner may engage in explaining what they are doing to others, seeking immediate support by working out loud and gaining input from those around them. This is a kind of sharing, but not as deliberate as that found in

FIGURE **10.1** The informal learning model plus Jarche's seek-sense-share

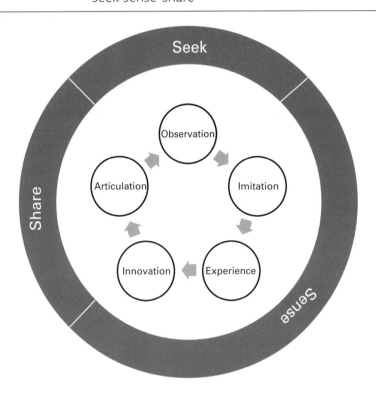

the final stage, when the informal learner reflects on what they have done and shares their learning with others. This fulfils a two-fold purpose:

1 It creates artefacts that may support others who may need to complete similar tasks and address similar problems in the future; and

2 It forces a process of reflection that deepens the learning and supports the embedding of this knowledge for the individual.

For seek-sense-share to work in an organizational context, there may need to be a further overlay of organizational inputs:

In this further expanded version of the model (Figure 10.2), we can see how the employer has a series of activities in which they should engage:

Signpost: As a minimum, the organization should point those requiring additional skills and knowledge to sources of information and advice. This may include maintaining a platform that houses this information and facilitating

FIGURE 10.2 Informal learning continuum plus personal knowledge management plus organizational actions

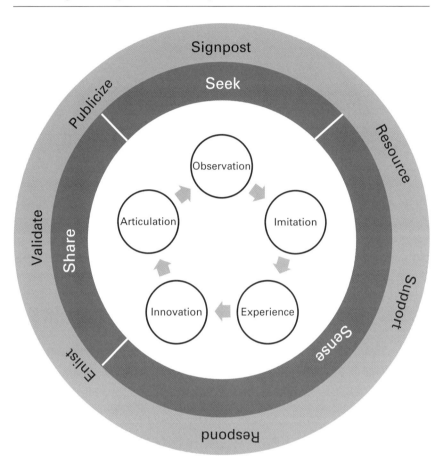

search activities by those wishing to find out more. This does not preclude the use of Google or other search engines and access to the World Wide Web, but the organization gains no competitive advantage from its personnel merely accessing the information that many other commercial organizations have chosen to make freely available. Some information should reflect a company's intellectual property and unique capabilities.

Resource: If individual employees are to take the risk of trying something new, the organization may need to provide resources to encourage this process of trial and error. This may be as simple as providing an opportunity to use the new idea, knowledge or process before it is forgotten. As we saw in Chapter 8, those organizations that expect coaching to take place but do not provide sufficient management resources for coaching to be a realistic possibility are failing to live up to the promises they make to employees. Enterprises also need to allow occasional failures in real live situations. In a manufacturing operation, for example, junior staff trying out new manufacturing approaches may create additional waste. Customer service teams may take slightly longer to deal with customer queries. Average performance scores may dip. The short-term costs of doing things more slowly and learning from mistakes must be weighed against the longer-term benefits of increased capability.

Support: As well as support via the line manager or the more knowledgeable and experienced team member, the process requires active support in dealing with those who may struggle in their initial attempts to try to do things differently. Often we see new skills and approaches abandoned in favour of the tried and tested simply because a little encouragement is lacking at the lowest moments. Enabling peers to come together who may all be struggling with the same issues can remove any sense of isolation or particular hopelessness. If everyone is feeling the strain, sharing the sense of frustration can be cathartic and energizing for the next push towards the mastery of new skills.

Of course in a networked world this does not need to be face to face. Assuming some kind of connection has already been established, bringing people together in facilitated online groups can be a great alternative to racking up the air miles or even negotiating the room booking calendar in the corporate HQ. The pre-existing connection seems to make a difference. Where a connection exists in the real world this would appear to reduce performative posturing in the online space. To share real learning and to discuss areas of difficulties openly requires a degree of authenticity that 'making a good impression' sometimes strips from our exclusively online interactions. The organization that gets this need for authentic, honest connections will have pump primed the webinar and the Google Hangout by first having people meet in the flesh.

Respond: As new skills and knowledge are being used with increasing expertise and frequency, the organization may need to respond. The first response is to acknowledge the new found capability and let people get on with things. Too often informally gained skills are not recognized and team members may be denied the opportunities and responsibilities that will enable them to grow in their role and develop the confidence required to own their new skills and knowledge. This is most effectively managed through a process of innovation – doing something new or applying the new knowledge in novel ways. This may not be new to the world, just new to the individual, team or even the wider enterprise. Organizations that provide the freedom to learners to work in new ways in a supportive environment garner significant benefits. Creativity is not only valuable to the organization in terms of improving performance or saving time and costs. Having the opportunity to use their creativity increases job satisfaction and employee engagement. This, in turn, increases staff loyalty and reduces regrettable staff turnover.

Enlist: If we want learners to utilize any kind of social network – there is a further qualification for recruits regarding their ability to use the available networks as engines of their own discovery-based practice. An individual's confidence with technology, including a degree of media literacy to ensure that not every tweet, blog and online article is uncritically accepted, should also factor into the selection process. At the innovation stage, learners may transfer from learner to learned and so we also need them to have the skills to share their knowledge.

There is a significant quality control issue here. Jaron Lanier, in his book *You Are Not A Gadget* takes issue with the prevailing idea that if we have enough contributors, the 'wisdom of crowds' will smooth out any lack of quality.[3] To intervene to promote some, higher-quality inputs to social networks would be perceived as inimical to many involved in the arguments centred on the democratization of the web. It is, as Lanier points out, wholly bogus to suggest there is a crowdsourced alternative to 'garbage in; garbage out'.

When discussing the so-called wisdom of crowds, Lanier says: 'Collectives can be just as stupid as any individual – and, in important cases, stupider.' He goes on: 'Every authentic example of collective intelligence that I am aware of also shows how that collective was guided or inspired by well-meaning individuals.' By enlisting those well-meaning individuals to spark a debate or to sow a seed, the organization has made an attempt to reduce the amount of ill-informed opinion in favour of a more structured and useful discussion anchored in real experience and founded on sound principles.

Validate: I was unsure about including validation in this list of organizational activities until I met with the team at LV= which I described in Chapter 5. The process within their Resolv= platform in which customer service representatives asked questions that could be answered by anyone in the business, relied on experts endorsing or correcting the answers given. Insurance is a regulated market and rightly so, so the potential costs of providing – however innocently – potentially misleading information could be enormous. In LV='s case having a checking process is essential for them to continue to receive a clean bill of health from the regulator. However, even in less well regulated situations a validation process enables individuals who have developed expertise that they are prepared to share to be recognized. The validation exercise also enables further learning needs to be assessed. If a simple question posted in a forum generates several misleading or simply wrong answers, that's information which needs to be acted upon.

Publicize: Finally, the process requires a certain concentration of resources around telling people what is there. Done right, this is part of the recognition and reward strategy for those who have contributed as well as promoting a solution that is designed to reduce calls to the help desk and speed time to competence.

CASE STUDY SABMiller plc

Of course telling people about the existence of a platform is not sufficient on its own. Global brewer SABMiller plc has an internal Yammer community focused on the corporate affairs teams working in areas related to regulation and managing and responding to societal expectations. They call it Licence to Trade which they define as 'the permission of society to continue to manufacture and sell alcohol'.

The teams across the globe that are involved in managing Licence to Trade interact with many different stakeholders. Governments have the power to restrict sales or marketing activities and can increase prices through higher excise tax. Local communities can take issue with the company for increases in abusive consumption and its implications, other producers can behave in ways that damage the reputation of the whole category. Their own colleagues in marketing and advertising may plan a major campaign that would attract criticism from special interest groups or local communities. The job of the Licence to Trade managers is to assist the individual companies that make up the world's second largest beer company to navigate the concerns of society, the needs of government and the commercial realities of continuing profitability.

The situation with regard to Licence to Trade (LTT) is different in each country. Different economic requirements means that beer is sometimes celebrated, sometimes demonized and heavily taxed. Different societal pressures mean that attitudes to alcohol consumption can vary enormously. The financial predicament of individual states can significantly change a government's attitude to alcohol taxation.

The Licence to Trade Yammer platform enables individuals to share experiences and ask questions of the global community. Each specific topic – marketing restrictions, taxation etc – has a global champion who oversees what is going on in each forum. They have enlisted experts not only from the global centre, but from regions and end markets as well. There is a meritocratic approach to the monitoring and management of the platform.

However, gaining contributions from across the 75 countries in which SABMiller operates has not been easy. The business language of the company is English and the Yammer community works primarily in English. Individuals involved in the programme from South America (for example) will be expected to share information in a language that will almost certainly not be their first language and may indeed not even be their second language. This is a huge barrier for those from primarily non-English speaking regions in relation to their engagement with the Yammer community. Not being confident in written English reduces their willingness to act as generators of content and sharers of experience.

There are ways around this and many individuals will utilize existing documentation to tell the story of the successful lobbying campaign or the programme of training for bar tenders that reduced alcohol abuse or drink driving. These existing documents will be board-level reports explaining what happened to the resources that have been devoted to the initiative. Recognizing that time with the senior team is at a premium, the reports are heavy on results and short on the process by which the results were achieved. They fulfil the purpose of providing management information very well, but their role as learning resources are limited.

In promoting the use of Yammer, the SABMiller team created a series of videos. These were deliberately low tech. All of them were filmed on smartphones or recorded from video calls using Skype. The idea was to model the behaviour in which people shared the detailed steps of what they had been doing in as immediate a fashion as possible. There was no requirement to produce a grammatically perfect report to help others understand the context, the challenge and the options pursued. It was a process of content generation that was as simple – if not simpler – than editing for wider consumption the last LTT manager's report to the board.

It also means that those encouraged to share their stories are not limited to explaining the good news that inevitably feature significantly in the quarterly reports to the executive committee. The short, low tech videos can be a route to sharing things that didn't go quite as well as hoped. 'This is about sharing information, sharing data and sharing success stories. It's also about sharing failures because we have those too and there's lots to be learned from them,'

Kirstin Wolfe, SABMiller plc's head of global industry affairs told me. She went on: 'We can record these case studies just by taking an iPhone and making a video and sharing it out with the group. That's something we haven't been able to do before.'

Gaining the benefits of user-generated content

This marriage of the immediacy of mobile technology and the advances in these areas, with some fundamental skills in selecting the right people and engaging them in telling their stories is the heart of how social networks can fulfil their dual roles in organizational learning.

- The first role is to provide a searchable database of lessons learned that individuals can interrogate and use as the starting point of looking for information and answers to questions.

- The second role, and I would argue much more important one, is to create an imperative for individuals to reflect on what they have experienced, document what worked and what didn't and summarize their own learning. The reflective role of social media is often overlooked in favour of the bells and whistles of re-tweets, likes and followers. One person writing a blog or contributing to a wiki that helps that individual make sense of what they have experienced is sufficient to render some social media-based learning experiences worthwhile. If that reflective process can also be recognized, then so much the better. Remember: what gets measured, gets done.

Smile – you're on TV

It is worth reflecting on SABMiller's focus on video. These are primarily 'talking head' videos in which an individual tells a story. The video may be a more efficient way of gathering the insights and packaging them for digital consumption, but they are still an explanation by someone of what has happened and, hopefully, the skills that would be useful in a similar situation in the future. In the informal learning model this is different from 'observation' and has less impact than actually watching a skilled individual perform a task.

Now, it is fair to say that not everything we may need people to learn informally at work will need a demonstration of the different steps and the chance to watch someone doing their work. In many cases observing a task being undertaken would be both dull and an inefficient use of time.

However for some skills, actually watching someone do something can be invaluable. There is a new route for this within the world of social media and user generated content: the instructional videos posted on YouTube and similar video sharing sites. YouTube is now the second most used search engine in the world and this cannot only be explained by an insatiable demand for funny cat videos.[4] At the heart of this use of YouTube is a hunger to be shown how to do things in the same way as cookery, gardening and DIY shows have flourished on mainstream, broadcast TV. Certainly I have heard many anecdotes among people making things, completing their children's Mathematics homework assignments or solving design problems about turning to YouTube as a route to finding a solution to an immediate problem. It is a regularly used source of Just-In-Time learning.

Hamish is 22. He enjoys the slightly more unusual music festivals and as someone who likes to join in and is not afraid to have a go, he is learning firestaff. For the uninitiated this is a kind of extreme juggling with a pole, each end of which is alight. In the twilight in a field somewhere with the right kind of music it is truly spectacular.

Hamish has been trying to learn since seeing some expert fire performers. But he has no one immediately available to help him so he relies on instructional videos from You Tube. 'The trouble is,' he told me 'if you've got a problem you can't ask for help. Like for me, there's this move I'm trying and every time I get the staff on to my shoulder it falls off. I can't seem to get to the bottom of what I'm doing wrong.'

Hamish needs a feedback loop. Like traditional eLearning the instructional videos on YouTube have been made by subject matter experts many of whom can no longer remember exactly what it was like not to be able to do the things that they are demonstrating. The performative nature of the medium is that part of the appeal to making the video is to appear expert. The expertise that is coveted is in respect of the skill – in this case firestaff. Even if it were possible for there to be more step-by-step instruction – and I've rarely seen a YouTube instructional video that is particularly good in this regard – the performative appeal of the medium is not to be a teacher, but to be a celebrity or a star.

> Hamish is a dancer and has trained in ballet and contemporary dance since he was eight years old. He is used to moving his body rhythmically and completing complex moves. But when he trained as a dancer someone watched every move and gave him specific feedback. The marginal gains he required to be spelled out step by step were described to him. On YouTube, you're on your own and sometimes that's just not enough.

I think the jury is out on the extent to which this phenomenon is significant in relation to informal learning within organizations. Watching a video may be learning but it may also be very similar to consulting the instructions supplied with flat-pack furniture. It may be a source of new knowledge and skills and it could also be a driver for further unreflective copying as defined in Rahwan *et al* and discussed in Chapter 7. It may also be a source of discouragement, as without proper step-by-step instruction and a feedback loop providing specific insights into how you can do better, some skills are just too difficult to master.

It may be enough to notice that:

- Video is increasingly accessible and individuals seem prepared to access and create video using mobile devices. This means that there are many more opportunities for low cost, relatively disposable video to be part of an organization's informal learning resources. Creating the video is absolutely analogous with preparing a blog in that it requires reflection and enables learning resources to be generated directly by practitioners rather than by media teams or learning materials designers.

- Observation in the informal learning model is usually accompanied by an opportunity to ask questions and to gain feedback on one's faltering first steps towards imitation. This is not available from a remote video site. As well as creating a video demonstrating an internal process or procedure, it may be necessary for organizations to ensure that well trained people offering support and feedback are available for those who will attempt to imitate the steps they have been shown.

I have seen a number of so-called social learning sites that use video quite heavily. In fact, there are many demonstrations of sales managers, senior leaders and chief executives exhorting their troops to ever greater levels of effort and commitment to the corporate cause. These are not learning resources and shouldn't be confused with the real user generated materials discussed here. These are corporate communications, created in the same way they always were and featuring the same characters they always did. Whether they work or not is a matter for others who specialize in corporate communications and employee engagement. I only know that learning cannot be reduced to being told things by the boss.

Producing video lectures that replicate the classroom without the expense of attendance and the variability of different groups and different locations is not informal learning either. This is simply a reduced cost way of delivering the formal training that everyone agrees requires a bit of an overhaul. The one place where video lectures have certainly seen a new renaissance is in massive open online courses or MOOCs. For the most part these digital experiments by major universities are an interesting way of repackaging their formal programmes in a Zeitgeist-y Web 2.0 format. Despite this somewhat unpromising start point, I do think there are some real opportunities to learn how informal learning may be configured in future by looking at the experiences of those who use and provide MOOCs. That's where our journey takes us next.

Notes

1 Conner, M, Pontefract, D and Brown, K (2013) *Revolutionize Corporate Learning: Beyond formal, informal, mobile, social dichotomies*, Creative Commons, available at www.marciaconner.com/learning-nouveau [accessed 30 May 2015].

2 Davenport, T H (2011) Rethinking knowledge work: a strategic approach, *McKinsey Quarterly* (February).

3 Lanier, J (2011) *You Are Not A Gadget*, Penguin, London, p 56.

4 Elliott, A (2013) The second largest search engine, infographic, available at http://www.socialmediatoday.com/content/second-largest-search-engine-infographic [accessed 30 May 2015].

Learning from academia: MOOCs and the flipped classroom

11

Of course, not everyone utilizing social networks for learning is following a programme designed by their employer. The staggering numbers of individuals signing up for massive open online courses (MOOCs) shows a real hunger for self-managed learning among some groups – particularly in highly specialized areas where organizational learning could not expect to provide learning opportunities to match those provided by specialist academic centres.

MOOCs come in two flavours xMOOCs and cMOOCs. The xMOOC is the closest replication of undertaking a university-led course. Led by academics and experts in their field, they tend to contain a series of inputs led or curated by specialists in the field. For the most part enrolment is free and they certainly earn the M for massive as hundreds of thousands of individual students may be enrolled on each course. Typically lasting from 4 to 12 weeks, this kind of MOOC will be 'owned' by a particular academic institution. As with most free stuff available on the web, there is a commercial rationale as MOOC providers are hoping to use this presence to experiment and test different learning approaches that may be rolled out in the future courses – presumably to attract paying students in larger and larger numbers. The other commercial perspective is that they act as an advertisement for the institution. If you've signed up for a MOOC via Coursera, Udacity, EdX or FutureLearn you will be familiar with the kind of offering.

The cMOOC is designed primarily as a peer-to-peer learning experience with user involvement and connection being the primary driver for their existence. They were originated in Canada (Athabasca and Manitoba universities) and were originally designed as connectivist (from which the c is derived) learning experiences. A connectivist model enables individuals to learn through discussion with peers who are wrestling with similar concepts. Taking these debates and discussions online is, in many ways, a natural development. It is using communications technology to replicate and eventually replace activities that would formally have needed to be conducted face to face. The idea borrows significantly from ideas such as communities of practice in which skilled individuals work across organizational boundaries to collaborate on issues of common interest.

Although cMOOCs were originally designed to be predominately about online student interaction, moderated and supported by faculty staff, and xMOOCS were about disseminating content, over time, the xMOOC model has also included increasing opportunities for students to connect, comment and learn from each other.

My intention with this chapter is not to try to cut through the controversy and debates about the value of MOOCs or their role in the future academic landscape. Others are better placed to fulfil that role. I am interested in the degree to which these types of innovation present alternative models for organizational learning in the future and the demands that this will make on learners and L&D departments if they are to appropriately adapt these strategies to work-based learning.

Flipping the classroom

The rise of the MOOC as a feature on the educational and learning landscape builds on another academic experiment originally introduced at Harvard and then adopted by other US universities. The flipped classroom removes the lecture from the student experience and instead distributes recordings of lectures, presentations and reading to students. The students' time with lecturers and professors is then spent in debate, discussion and tutorial activity rather than in a large lecture theatre listening to a paper being delivered with little chance for interaction.

The technology for the dissemination of the materials included videos of lectures, voiced presentations as well as the usual academic literature. In many ways the flipped classroom is nothing new to those of us engaged in organizing learning at work. Blended learning (which I describe in more detail in Chapter 12) is a broadly similar idea. In blended programmes, technology is used to frontload information using online modules. This online 'pre-work' is followed by a shorter, more experiential workshop built on increased opportunities for group work between learners who now possess a common vocabulary and a shared level of understanding of the topic.

The flipped classroom has recently taken off across a number of institutions in the aftermath of MOOC creation. In one experiment, San Jose State University in California partnered with MOOC platform EdX. Eighty-five students were then given access to MOOC-style video lectures and attended class twice a week to practise the skills they had been shown in the videos and to ask questions of lecturers and peers. Mid-term exams results were noticeably better when compared with previous cohorts on the same course.[1] This kind of application is where I think universities will increasingly experiment with different teaching and learning methods in order to increase student numbers without an attendant increasing in resources. Those graduates you recruit in the next few years may be well used to this style of learning.

Clearly the flipped classroom and the xMOOCs could simply be viewed as alternative delivery methods for formal training. There is no real requirement for informal learning unless one considers undertaking prescribed academic reading or being directed to watch a video on YouTube as an informal activity. This seems to be very similar to completing an eLearning module which I think is pretty formal. Furthermore, like some of the compliance eLearning that abounds in organizations, if a certificate of completion is required, the use of each section needs to be completed within a specific timetable.

The implications for learners

One of the ways of thinking about MOOCs is as timetabled collections of learning resources. They are sources of information brought together in one place. They are also touted as democratizing access to education – in some articles I read the suggestion was made that this would extend University access to those in developing countries at a fraction of the cost.[2] Anant Agarwal, CEO of EdX and a professor at MIT wrote in the *Observer* in June 2013: 'MOOCs make education borderless, gender-blind, race-blind, class-blind and bank account-blind. Up to now, quality education – and in some cases any higher education at all – has been the privilege of the few. MOOCs have changed that.'[3]

Open education pioneer, Sir John Daniel, formerly of the Open University, would disagree, not least because he sees an unresolvable disconnect between promoting access to education among disadvantaged learners and making money: 'It is a myth to think that providing not-for-credit open online education from the USA will address the challenges of expanding higher education in the developing world.'[4]

I think organizations can learn something from the reaction of learners to being given access to lots of resources with few expectations about how much or when they consult these resources. There are interesting interplays between the content that is presented and the discussions that take place and the degree to which individual students engage in additional learning or research. In order to find out more, I became a MOOC student. I enrolled on the Global Food Security MOOC offered over eight weeks by Lancaster University via the FutureLearn platform.

As someone who is involved from time to time in producing learning resources, my initial reaction was that the production quality of some of the video resources left something to be desired. However, reservations were quickly overcome as the material that was being presented was just the right side of challenging. My interest in the topic, coupled with my lack of previous study in the area, enabled me to overcome any reservations.

I decided to become an active participant in the course and commented whenever asked to do so and once or twice entered into online conversations with other MOOC participants and the moderators of the forums. I also completed all assessments and commented on the assessments of others when this opportunity arose. I consulted all extra resources when these were available. I created a Tumblr blog and participated on social media using the relevant hashtags and links. I had allotted around four hours a week to the MOOC but I found it was taking anything up to 10 hours per week to complete to the level that I thought was useful and interesting for me.

In my assiduous use of the MOOC I was unusual. One of the various criticisms of MOOCs is that although many thousands of individual learners sign up for the courses, levels of dropout are extremely high. I don't have access to the figures for the MOOC I was involved in but it seemed there were relatively few names appearing repeatedly on the forums. That, of course, does not mean that people were no longer involved – just not publicly commenting on the various discussion boards.

Along with the amount of time I spent on the programme, the other clear learning was that the main benefit was in reading around the subject when my preconceptions were challenged. This was particularly the case when I engaged in conversations with other learners and needed to back up the points I was making. The resources provided by the Lancaster team became, for me and a few others who commented similarly, stimulus for some genuine informal learning through desk research and additional reading.

Others seemed less open to being convinced and with a subject like food security I guess it was inevitable that some who signed up would have strong and unwavering positions on some facets of the topic. The course featured a number of agricultural scientists and those engaged in genetic modification that raised particularly high levels of negative commentary among some. There was a group of learners who had a particular belief in a set of solutions to hunger based on traditional farming methods. They were vehemently opposed to anything that looked like factory farming, genetic modification or even, in some cases, the involvement of business and commerce in the process. Rarely, these individuals just decided the course wasn't for them. Their disengagement usually started with criticism of the course, the content, the interviewees and the academics involved. This progressed to attacks on the people who defended those involved and in a welter of immoderate comments and online arguments that generated more heat than light, they digitally flounced away from the course.

I was speaking at a conference recently with a group of people involved in IT education. The subject turned to using 'free' platforms to enable online collaboration between learners and within communities of practice.

I urged caution. Organizations should bear in mind that by using a twitter hashtag or a Facebook page or Google circle, the users don't need to be personally identified and could hide their identity. I recounted the story of Caroline Criado Perez who started a campaign to have an eminent female depicted on the back of a UK £10 note.

I asked those in attendance to tell me who was on the back of the £10 without looking in their wallets or purses. No one could come up with a name. Despite the fact that this was not something that had registered with most of us, Criado Perez was subject to significant abuse at the time of her campaign. At one stage, because she had the temerity to organize a petition asking for a woman to feature on a British banknote she received 50 rape threats per minute via Twitter!

My experience of the angry exchanges on the MOOC – although a thousand times more pleasant than this example – suggests that organizations need to keep control of their collaboration platforms and be able to act swiftly to remove anything that is bullying or abusive. Sounds common sense, but if an organization chooses to roll out an initiative using Twitter or Facebook, it can be extremely difficult to have the offending posts removed.

As a codicil to that story, Charles Darwin was eventually replaced with Jane Austen on the UK £10 note.

What was instructive about this was that this was akin to some of the discussions occasionally seen on newspaper articles about controversial subjects, religion or politics. Battle lines are drawn and the anonymity of one's digital profile provides a screen from behind which people choose to say things they would rarely if ever air in a face-to-face discussion. Although moderation ensured that the MOOC discussions were kept pretty tame by comparison, one could imagine the direction of travel had it been absent.

A free online course will attract a wide range of people. Some participants may not feel they need to learn very much and log on for very different reasons, perhaps to promote a viewpoint, or maybe to parade their existing knowledge. On the Food Security MOOC, there were many learners from around the world and, gratifyingly, a few from regions where food security issues caused by erosion, drought or floods are a daily reality. Those involved tended to have a pretty high level of prior experience and knowledge of the subject matter. Clearly this caused something of a headache for the people making the resources in knowing at which level to pitch the content. It was apparent from some of the online discussions that quite a few people believed the material to be too simple, for a minority of others, it was too advanced. The MOOC asked for no prior qualifications or experience and yet reading the profiles of a few regular contributors it was clear that many of them were already well qualified in food science, agriculture or international development, often to postgraduate level.

Perhaps this is one of the issues with open access materials for learners. Many informal learning advocates – and especially those promoting MOOCs and other online collaboration and content sharing platforms – see the open access as a positive, democratizing force in making learning available for everyone. In truth, however, the early adopters seem to be the informed and educated. If the individual is inherently motivated to learn about something, perhaps they already have taken those opportunities available? Early adopters are drawn from the ranks of the converted. If this is so, the MOOC becomes a poor model for addressing capability gaps in organizations.

Who uses MOOCs, how and why?

In a study of courseware analytics carried out by Stanford Lytics Lab[5] on three different computer science MOOCs, they found that learners could be categorized in one of four groups:

- Samplers: those who briefly explore the course by watching a few videos;

- Auditors: those who watched lectures throughout but completed few or none of the assignments;

- Disengaged: those who watched videos and completed assignments at the start but subsequently only watch lectures or disappear completely; and

- Completers: those who completed most of the assignments and watched the majority of videos.

In all three courses, the samplers were the biggest group with completers being the smallest, in many cases 10 per cent or fewer MOOC students were completers.

In a further study, Phil Hill,[6] an educational technologist, classified learners as Lurkers (similar to auditors), Passive Participants (Samplers) and Active Participants (Completers). He also has a group called Drop-ins who want to use only part of a MOOC, will take what they require and then skip the remainder of the course.

The most complete research on MOOC participation was provided by Edinburgh University. They collaborated with Coursera – the US based MOOC provider – on six MOOCs in early 2013. Their subsequent report about that experience was extremely illuminating.[7]

As with any 'free' experience the number of those signing up for the programmes was significantly higher than the number of those actually starting the courses. However, around 53 per cent of those who registered did become active learners at some point in the process: that is; they accessed the specific MOOC course site within the Coursera platform and agreed to the terms and conditions of use. In total, this was an impressive figure of over 165,000 learners. As with my personal, but perhaps unrepresentative, MOOC experience, the educational attainment level of those who did participate (or at least completed questionnaires about their experience) was somewhat higher than anticipated. Five of the MOOCs were targeted at those with similar educational attainment levels to an undergraduate student (the Artificial Intelligence Planning MOOC was a postgraduate course) and yet around 70 per cent of total enrolments were from people with graduate level or postgraduate level qualifications.

Unlike on other online courses provided by Edinburgh University, involvement in the MOOC did not require engagement with forums and social networks, although each course could use the Coursera forum areas. The report says: 'All Edinburgh MOOCs chose to retain the optional quality of the forums, noting that forum discussions are not necessarily comfortable activities for all participants, especially if they are new to online learning environments.'[8]

Although optional, there were a number of unusual and innovative uses of social networking on these MOOCs and to support the forums and networks, teaching assistants (TAs) were recruited to support learners. The academic staff and TAs were given training by the university's Institute for Academic Development (IAD). This training included media skills (for creating video – a significant feature of all the MOOCs) and a community of practice enabling the TAs and academics to offer support to one another as issues occurred through the programmes.

Dr Louise Connelly of the IAD explained to me that the role of TAs and academics obviously involved some monitoring of threads and discussions forums for inappropriate content. As discussed above, on an open access site this is a base line requirement. But as well as the relatively minor policing role, it was important to help learners deal with the potentially overwhelming amount of commentary on the various forums. Dr Connelly told me: 'Although we expect TAs and academics on the forums to post questions and help get discussions going, in reality the discussions are already pretty lively before the official start of the forum. By the time the TA gets on to the site, the discussion is already well under way and conversations have emerged. The role then changes to summarizing, keeping things on track, helping structure the discussions boards so people keep together. A weekly Google hangout (live webcam/video sessions involving university staff in summarizing themes and responding to learner comments over the preceding period) helps people clarify the main themes.'

I checked out some of the recorded outcomes of these sessions – from Google Hangouts to Twitterchats and other synchronous and asynchronous interactions between MOOC participants. As Louise Connelly said, they can be pretty overwhelming – the volume of posts and commentary is initially difficult to make sense of and ranges from the logistical and administrative to the philosophical. But one eventually becomes able to make sense of some of the themes within different discussions. What really struck me was that there was a significant ('overwhelming') level of interaction but actually very few active learners were participating. This is not in any way a criticism of the Edinburgh MOOC – as they explicitly set out to make engagement with these social networks a voluntary, optional exercise. However, the numbers of these highly technologically savvy learners, who were voluntarily taking a course in an area of personal or professional interest, were comparatively low. The highest proportion of learners posting about their learning was in the Equine Nutrition course in which 32 per cent of learners participated. In Artificial Intelligence Planning, just 4 per cent of students got involved (although this group could also collaborate within Second Life and the number who did was not tracked or reported).

In the eLearning and Digital Cultures course – a group that one would have expected to embrace social networks with a vengeance – only 12 per cent were active on the forums. That said, there were very many other options for them to interact – through Twitter, Facebook, Google+ and Google Hangouts. But from almost 22,000 active participants, 4,820 joined the learner-led Facebook group, 1,945 engaged in the learner-led, Google+ group, there were approximately 700 tweets per day using the hashtag #edcmooc. One of the twitterchats using the hashtag #edcmchat generated upwards of 700 tweets per hour when live, but in each instance involved fewer than 90 participants. There were 915 blogs created – or one for every 23 active students.

Now I think these numbers are remarkable – they are very significant levels of social network use for the sole purpose of individuals learning through sharing their experiences and engaging with others who are similarly enthused. But many more of those enrolled – even in a course called eLearning and Digital Cultures – are either passively engaged, reading what others put but not contributing themselves, or not engaged at all. With all the support available, having devoted time to ensure that academics and TAs were participating in and supporting learners to use forums and other web 2.0 tools, the Edinburgh MOOCs were 'overwhelmed' by the active contribution of at most, 20 per cent of active student numbers.

Can you build your own MOOC (and would you want to)?

I think my experience as a MOOC student, the analytics of user numbers and participation rates and the data that has been published by Edinburgh University and others suggest that creating a MOOC-style intervention for work based learning will not be an initiative taken lightly. Creating resources, maintaining the platform, moderating comments and recruiting (and training) teaching assistants or mentors to support learners and filter content will be a significant commitment for an organization. MOOCs are currently optional for those who use them; I have found no studies of what happens when involvement is required or mandatory. To some extent requiring an employee to become involved in a MOOC would be counter intuitive. It would go against the whole design process and be, ultimately, self-defeating. Without some assuredness of how many employees would use the MOOC-like platform it would seem a risky and possibly an expensive proposition.

Despite these caveats, I still think that organizations could engender a different approach to learning by looking at some of the MOOC characteristics. I'm not certain that there is a lot new in the concept of the MOOC or of flipping learning. Many educators would claim good teachers and lecturers have been doing this kind of thing for decades, but without the fancy technology to enable students with iPads to get involved.

In organizational learning, the idea of collaboration and communities of practice are central to Situated Learning. Situated Learning was first discussed by social anthropologist, Jean Lave and Etienne Wenger, an expert on artificial intelligence, in their 1991 study 'Situated Learning: Legitimate peripheral participation'. Lave and Wenger argue that learning primarily takes place in the environment in which it is practised. Etienne Wenger has described these communities as 'tribes learning to survive'[9] that certainly locates the learning practice they observed and documented within a historical context. In their purest form, communities of practice hark back to pre-history.

But it would be disingenuous to ignore the potential expansion of these types of shared learning endeavours that technology affords the modern organization. The game has been changed by 24-hours-a-day connectivity and the potential for anyone to create and distribute information, reflections, research and opinion. There's no point being in denial about the power and ubiquity of communications technology.

To start let's look at the characteristics of the MOOC and flipped learning that may inform organizational practice. I call these the 6 Cs:

- Create
- Curate
- Culture
- Communicate
- Collaborate, and
- Community

Create

The starting point is to create some resources. Typically in university and school settings these have been video lectures. Research by Guo, Kim and Rubin[10] found that short videos are preferred (about six minutes) and that they are received well by learners when they are specifically made for the course. Interestingly, the videos in which instructors speak quickly and are obviously enthusiasts were found to be significantly more engaging. Authenticity is important for a more media literate audience. According to Guo, Kim and Rubin, this extends to the professionalism of the finished product. More polished productions are less well received than the more personal feel achieved by filming on smartphones, tablets or recording from Skype.

A word of warning

Video pictures can look a little grainy or the lighting not be terrific, but make sure the sound is good! Whenever I've participated in programmes using home produced video, the negative comments have always been about the sound quality.

Podcasts (audio recordings) and other media such as whiteboard videos, slide shows, blogs and documents would also need to be created. Throughout, brevity seems to be the watchword. Putting online a two-hour lecture filmed by a single camera at the back of the lecture hall is unlikely to be well received. Or, for that matter, watched.

Whatever resources are created, the indexing and tagging of those resources is incredibly important. There is no point in having endless resources created that share knowledge across the organization if no one in the organization can find what they need when they need it. This can't be left to technologists ignorant of the subjects covered or the roles that people will be undertaking when access to the resources is needed. While it is perfectly sensible to borrow from the MOOCs and make the resources initially available in clusters – appended to levels or weeks – they also need to be capable of being searched for and accessed (or re-accessed) in an ad hoc, just-in-time basis. This is one reason not to leave your MOOC-like collaborative learning platform to your existing LMS. Despite the claims of your LMS vendor I have never seen either a learning management system or learning and content management system that can handle open access to the resources that it houses. There are always limitations or difficulties in linking one item to another or finding something embedded in the LMS-driven course structure.

Curate

The alternative to creating your own content is to mine the web for existing, freely available content. Curation is a key activity within the context of learning based around social networks. Helping individuals make sense of what Dr Louise Connelly at Edinburgh University described to me as 'overwhelming' levels of content is an essential. Trawling through the potentially never-ending amount of information available to your learners is time intensive. Without a degree of filtering and quality control, the results of endless web-searches may throw up information that may be unreliable, under-researched or simply wrong. As we saw in Chapter 7, you can't necessarily believe everything you read on the internet, regardless of how many times it has been retweeted or liked!

The quality-control mechanism introduces another idea into the mix. A curator not only shares information but tacitly endorses it as well. The curator cannot be a 21-year-old intern who 'knows how to use a search engine'. A curator will need significant experience both of the subject matter and as a learner.

Curation is a problematic word. In the past I have scorned its use. I think one of the reasons for its ascendancy is because it sounds sexier than librarian, which is what most of the role most closely resembles. As with other social media terms it is also prone to devaluation due to horrendous overuse. When I see someone described on the end credits of a film as 'the curator of music' – ie the person who chose the soundtrack that no one can remember from the movie but will appear on the cynically marketed spin-off album – then my concern seems justified.

Writer of *Curationism*, David Balzer reported how Lakehead Superior State University in Michigan has 'placed "curator", "curated" and "to curate" on its 2015 list of banished words.'[11] I hate to disappoint but the word starts with C and I do enjoy occasional alliteration.

This expertise is not necessarily fixed. When collaborating to share knowledge with peers (dictionary definition: someone equal to another in abilities, qualifications, age, background, and social status) that peer-level equality is not constant. What happens in reality is the rapid switching of positions of expertise. When sharing an experience, research, or case study, the person with the story is 'the expert' or authoritative voice. When listening, synthesizing and reflecting we are the student. The fact that in another moment those roles may be reversed in no way undermines the concept that for that period of time – however brief – someone fulfils the role of more knowledgeable other, which I first discussed in Chapter 7.

The more knowledgeable other (or MKO) is a key role within the concept of social constructivism defined by Vygostky almost 100 years ago.[12] The term is self-explanatory – a more knowledgeable other knows more about something. It usually denotes a professional educator – a teacher or trainer. But Vygotsky himself was clear that the MKO could be a peer – even in his studies that focused on young children. A child who already knew how to ride a bike or make a jigsaw could instruct his or her peer in mastering the self-same skills.

In this way, initially curation may be undertaken by someone known as a subject matter expert. As the resources are accessed and individuals undertake their own exploration of and around the topic, they too can recommend, signpost and endorse resources that they have found useful.

The initial curatorial role is another time intensive activity and an organization wishing to provide access to resources in support of increased organizational capability, need to budget appropriately for someone to undertake this role.

Culture

In Chapter 6 I described culture as 'the way we do things around here' or – more properly – 'the way we **should** do things around here.' This extends to learning. One of the challenges of informal learning that relies on the internet or computer technology is that it can appear similar to staff frittering away work time on YouTube. The creation of 'edutainment' style videos can be seen as trivial by some. Any restriction – whether explicit in instructions from manager or supervisor – or implicit in the rolled eyes and looks of disapproval – runs the risk of undermining the drive towards enabling individuals to take responsibility for their own learning.

This is one area of culture that has a top-down component. The senior staff of the organization will need to publicly endorse the approach and team leaders and departmental heads will need to be fully briefed on what it is, how it works and an acceptable amount of work time that can be spent using the platform. Making all access to the platform something that has to be undertaken in an employee's own time is discriminatory. Those with caring responsibilities, workers who are already under pressure and taking work home at weekends and evenings and those working shifts are much less likely to be able to use these resources than the single, younger employee working nine to five.

Communicate

A resource-based collaboration site, will not get used just because you have made it available. You'll need to tell people about it in a rolling campaign. The launch will be important, but all these kinds of initiatives in which I have ever been involved have started with a great deal of enthusiasm and then interest has tailed off pretty quickly. The communication process starts with initial launch, releases more news and information when new functionality or new resources are available and shares success stories from users when up and working.

Communication should also be direct and personal. When people comment on items on the platform make sure someone is acknowledging that and entering into a meaningful discussion. (Avoid the 'Thanks for the great comment' style verbiage. The more noise is created the less anyone listens.)

Use this communication process to link people together as well. If a person has commented on a topic, reply and tell them that you are directing other people to their comment who may also find it useful. There's an element of engineering the network going on here. This is valid. Too many good initiatives fall into disrepute because too few people adopt and use them in the medium term. It takes work to build and maintain momentum.

It goes without saying that communication should include not only the key target employees, but their supervisors and managers as well. This is part of making the continuous culture of collaboration business as usual and it is what these platforms must rely on if they are to deliver benefits.

Collaborate

This brings me neatly to the fifth of my Cs – collaborate. There are two different kinds of collaboration of relevance when thinking about adapting a MOOC-style approach to the organizational context.

The first is **content collaboration**. This is the kind of collaboration much utilized in some MOOCs that set assignments. Unsurprisingly, with potentially thousands of students, there is no offer by faculty staff to mark individual assignments in a free MOOC. The next best thing is for participants to post their assignments – usually a short essay or blog-length reflection on the course – to the platform and for other participants to provide feedback. Given the very wide range of students this is not always especially useful for the person submitting the assignment. With particularly inventive essays or reflections that resonate with the person providing feedback, there may be some benefits in reviewing someone else's work, but these are far from guaranteed. Instead the job becomes an administrative task over-laid and slightly separate from the learning which only those with a clear completer mind-set would bother with. I spoke to a couple of postgraduate students recently who told me this kind of peer reviewing was now incorp-orated into their course work. I can see some benefits of reviewing the work of others, especially where developing academic writing skills was one of the programme outcomes. However, the feedback received was rarely inci-sive and far too politely positive to provide the kind of insight that might result in a learning breakthrough. Tempting though it might be to create collaboration around learning tasks, reflections and assignments, I see little benefit in the organizational sphere, except perhaps as a way to ensure that tasks are completed. There are other more direct ways of doing this and they would be less time consuming.

The second type is **contextual collaboration**. These collaborations happen when learners work together to solve a problem or address a challenge. Those that have most impact are projects that are real and which the indi-viduals have a stake in addressing. Using your platform as a kind of project/issue dating agency has enormous benefits.

For example: Terri works in Vancouver and needs to pull together some house rules for the use of social media by company marketing teams. She posts in the 'help wanted' area of the collaborative platform. She also tags the post – perhaps with social media, marketing and policy. This means that any user of the system who is also interested in these three areas and anyone responsible for another project that shares one or more of these tags, is instantly alerted to Terri's requirement.

Joe is in Britain. He is working in brand marketing and he has already set up some social media house rules for the digital advertising agency that he works with.

Terri can now review Joe's house rules, adapt and adopt those that are useful and critique the rules for Joe so that he can amend them in the future. The whole process can be documented so that the original version, Terri's amended version and the revised version that Joe adopts can be posted as examples for anyone else looking for something similar.

Terri and Joe should each also write a blog, reflecting on the process, identifying the things they have learned and why they chose to make the amends they made. Incidentally, I would require anyone using the project collaboration area of the platform to agree to post a blog about the process and its outcomes – good or bad – on the platform.

This kind of contextual collaboration locates the learning in the workplace and involves an element of 'working out loud' that I'll discuss in more detail in the next chapter.

Community

Community also has two dimensions. The first is the community of practice. This is a group of individuals with a common interest, sharing ideas and discussing matters of co-concern. The idea of collaboration is not implicit in a community of practice although collaboration often follows.

There are a couple of issues with communities of practice that people sometimes overlook.

1 Everyone is not equal. Communities of practice often create their own hierarchy based on experience, renown or other less easily identifiable ideas. At the Online Educa conference in Berlin in late 2014, Howard Rheingold, author of *Netsmart, How to Survive Online*, coined the term peeragogy during his keynote address. He defined it as a new learning paradigm. Rheingold's breakthrough suggestion of how he did this was to always address his students as 'esteemed co-learners.' Maybe he is simply using the terminology of the collaborative age – after all, he is the TED talker, the visiting professor and the person behind the eponymous Rheingold U on which most of his co-learners were enrolled. It is unlikely that they truly believed his co-learner credentials. But behind Rheingold's professed humility he is acknowledging a universal truth. We are all created equal and we are all learners. But effective learning from one another requires someone – for however brief or prolonged a period – to be more expert than others. Communities of practice recognize this, however tacitly. New entrants or novices are given some opportunities to interact and contribute, but their role is primarily questioning and listening. The more experienced inner circle will be the ones collaborating. Professional institutes recognize this with their different membership bands, associate, member, fellow etc.

2 A broadly based community of practice is a hotbed of conflict, intrigue and disagreement. As we saw in Chapter 9, a 'me-shaped world' can be rather narrow and lead to significant blind spots in our learning of, and around, a subject. A good community of practice has the confidence to attract members who do not necessarily agree with each other and to encourage debates during which the areas of

conflict and disagreement are given an airing. In some online communities of the like-minded that I have seen, disagreement is actively discouraged. One of the challenges is that the discussion in the backchannel of a webinar or during a tweetup relies on very short, instant message length contributions. It is difficult to be nuanced, referenced and accurate in one's disagreement in 140 characters. I believe it is one of the reasons so many of the world's perpetually outraged are on Twitter. Microblogging allows only black and white opinions. Ambiguity and shades of grey are bleached out in favour of the absolutism of brevity.

The second dimension is what I would call the enterprise community. These communities are engaged in a common endeavour by virtue of being part of the same organization. Although individuals may have different responsibilities and expertise, the community still matters if they are pursuing the same mission and working with the same values. In my experience, values driven organizations that exist to do something more than simply enrich the shareholders tend to be slightly more successful in this area. Those that are primarily about financial success tend towards internal competition in a way that is detrimental to sharing and learning. If the only common feature is to make the pie as large as possible, don't be surprised if community learning is subservient to the battle to obtain the largest slice.

CASE STUDY The non-academic experience
MOOCPro and Curatr

In October 2014 I enrolled in another MOOC called Innovating Your Training Business. It was designed and delivered by Sam Burroughs and Martin Couzins from MOOCPro.co.uk and housed on the Curatr platform.[13] Curatr is the brainchild of Ben Betts who originally came up with the basics of the platform while studying at Warwick University. Essentially it provides a community space that can house a series of content items and links to related information around the web.

The Innovating Your Training Business MOOC was a free programme structured around levels. Each level covered a specific topic and content items within each level were ranked as essential, recommended and additional, enabling those with a particular interest in a topic to delve deeper. The programme also offered points, with a progression from level to level governed by the points accumulated. By watching videos, consulting resources and commenting on items you had seen you gained points – although there was no quality control on the comments made. A smiley face was sufficient to assure progression.

At certain points – roughly every second level – a gate appeared and access beyond the gate was denied until a short reflection had been entered. Once again this was not quality controlled but at least made an attempt to engineer some kind of online community building. To an extent it worked. Despite my cynicism of the 'Gee, this is really great!' style comments on sites like these, some were genuinely insightful, constructively critical and thoughtful responses to the comments made. The points tally was displayed in a leader board. At first I was prepared to dismiss this as patronising and a little childish. But it was spookily addictive. Trying to get myself up the leader board became a distraction from my other work. That might just be my competitive streak showing through but I was surprised at just how well this simple trick worked.

Over 350 people participated in the MOOC and the content took the participants through 15 levels covering everything from lean and agile thinking to communities and collaboration. From my highly personal viewpoint of a learner who has many years' experience in learning technologies, I did learn things. Mostly I learned about some technologies I didn't know about and primarily I learned about how Curatr works, which I guess was the commercial rationale behind the programme.

I didn't, however, change my position on any of the basic tenets of learning technologies, how they work and how individuals collaborate online. Was I supposed to? I'm not sure. I actively disagreed with some of the comments made by others and some of the contents of the curated items to which we were directed. I voiced my alternative views in the spaces available for comments (gaining points as I did so) though the extent to which these were read by others I'm not sure. I didn't spend a significant amount of time scrolling through the comments sections myself. For one thing the screen layout and the need to scroll, doesn't make these particularly accessible. The intention had been to promote comments that were rated by other users so that the 'most useful' rose to the top. In practice, insufficient comments were made – particularly on the additional or recommended sections – and not many users voted for the most useful comments. Where lots of comments were made they were mostly unmediated and simply displayed in date order.

Like the angry food security fundamentalists in the Food Security MOOC perhaps I was the wrong learner there for the wrong reasons. I hope I wasn't as boorish as some involved in my Lancaster MOOC experience whose sole purpose for being there was to promote a specific viewpoint, but I can see how it happens. I can see how attractive it might be to turn the safe space for a debate and an exchange of views into a gladiatorial contest between theories and positions. It would have meant capitalizing the space on the platform, indeed hijacking it from its original purpose towards an opportunity to get on my soap box and proclaim the gospel according to Hoyle. If I wasn't mindful of the learning requirements of others and the desire to promote an open and open-minded debate I could have responded to the urge to 'put everyone right'.

I think we have to accept that some people entering learning exercises like this are determined not to have their views changed. The process of change is uncomfortable. Voluntarily to enter into a space that requires me to experience discomfort is something most people would not do (Formula 1 bosses, notwithstanding). I can see how learners in those spaces, being asked to accept uncomfortable new information can battle with it, reject it, justify their rejection and – ultimately – disengage from the experience. It seems that changing people's behaviour – especially behaviour entrenched in the world of 'this is the way we've always done things' will require something more challenging than the softly, softly, collaborative debate of the professional MOOC.

Conclusion

The MOOC idea, whether as a utopian pedagogic experiment of connectivity and community based learning or as a route to publishing content in a platform in which large numbers of students can access the content, comment and connect with others with similar interests, is one that is too large to ignore for those interested in informal learning.

Resource banks of material that our employees can access, create, comment on and use seem to me to be positive opportunities for informal learning, but only if an organization has the resources to make it work. This is not a simple route to generating learning opportunities for staff. However, the routes to guided discovery that a MOOC-like platform provides for organizations and their employees are potentially of great interest.

In the Towards Maturity Infocus report about MOOCs in 2014 the report's authors focused on six key characteristics of MOOCs and noted that many of the organizations that came in the top 10 per cent of their annual n = benchmark survey were already using many of them.[14] Specifically, there was a big difference in use of what Towards Maturity referred to as collaborative technology – blogs, wikis, learning communities, communities of practices and in-house social media. The top learning companies were already using these features more than their lower performing counterparts. However, in any of these measures no more than the highest score – for the use of social media sites – was 61 per cent, meaning that of the top performing companies for their use of learning technology in the survey, almost 40 per cent do not have any framework for even using external, free social media as a part of the organizational learning offering. There is significant work to do if these technologies are to become the mainstream in organizational learning.

Encouraging involvement will not only deepen the learning experience for those who post blogs, comments and share information through the platform, it will also help the organization to spot those who may be supported to take on a mentoring or guide role, similar to the teaching assistants trained by the IAD at Edinburgh University for their MOOCs. If, through this involvement, people also generate, discover or curate additional resource of use for others in the organization, terrific, but I wouldn't make this the focus of their engagement. It is much more important to concentrate on each individual pulling what learning they can from the available resources followed by active encouragement for them to apply what they have learned to their work. Looking at how individuals can also learn seamlessly through the work they are doing, is the subject of the next chapter.

Notes

1 *Chronicle of Higher Education* (2012) San Jose State U. says replacing live lectures with videos increased test scores, chronicle.com, 17 October 2012, available at http://chronicle.com/blogs/wiredcampus/san-jose-state-u-says-replacing-live-lectures-with-videos-increased-test-scores/40470 [accessed 2 June 2015].

2 For a balanced critique of this approach see: http://www.slate.com/articles/technology/future_tense/2013/11/developing_countries_and_moocs_online_education_could_hurt_national_systems.html [accessed 2 June 2015].

3 Agarwal, A (2013) Online universities – time for teachers to join the revolution, *Observer*, Tech Monthly, 16 June 2013, available at http://www.theguardian.com/education/2013/jun/15/university-education-online-mooc [accessed 30 May 2015].

4 Daniel, J (2012) Making sense of MOOCs: musings in a maze of myth, paradox and possibility, *Journal of Interactive Media in Education* 3 (18), DOI: http://dx.doi.org/10.5334/2012-18.

5 Kizilcec, R, Piech, C and Schneider, E (2013) Deconstructing Disengagement, LyticsLab@Stanford, available at http://lytics.stanford.edu/deconstructing-

disengagement/. Quoted in Haggard S *et al* (2013) The Maturing of the MOOC, research paper, UK Department of Business and Skills (September).

6 Hill, P (2013) Emerging student patterns in MOOCs: a graphical view, e-Literate, 6 March 2013, available at http://mfeldstein.com/emerging_student_patterns_in_moocs_graphical_view/ [accessed 30 May 2015].

7 University of Edinburgh (2013) MOOCs@Edinburgh 2013 report #1, 10 May 2013, MOOCs@Edinburgh Group.

8 University of Edinburgh (2013), p 22.

9 Etienne Wenger 2007 quoted in infed.org (nd) Jean Lave, Etienne Wenger and communities of practice, available at http://infed.org/mobi/jean-lave-etienne-wenger-and-communities-of-practice/ [accessed 2 June 2015].

10 Guo, P J, Kim, J and Rubin, R (2014) How video production affects student engagement: an empirical study of MOOC videos, EdX (March), available at https://www.edx.org/blog/how-mooc-video-production-affects [accessed 30 May 2015].

11 Balzer, D (2015) 'Reading lists, outfits, even salads are curated – it's absurd', *Guardian*, 18 April 2015, available at http://www.theguardian.com/books/2015/apr/18/david-balzer-curation-social-media-kanye-west [accessed 2 June 2015].

12 A good primer on Vygotsky's ideas is Moll, L C (2013) *L S Vygotsky and Education*, Routledge (Key ideas in Education), London.

13 You can find out more here: http://www.curatr3.com/.

14 Overton, L (2014) Using MOOCs to transform traditional training, Towards Maturity (May), available at www.towardsmaturity.org/in-focus/MOOC2014 [accessed 30 May 2015].

SECTION THREE
Learning as you work, working as you learn

There are two holy grails of learning and development – if you can have two holy grails. The first involves being able to closely align the learning and development activities in an organization with the strategic goals of the organization.

The second is concerned with closely linking developmental inputs with behaviour and performance. It seems to me that the real interest in informal learning is that it potentially delivers in both these areas. But it can only really be said to do so if the informal learning that employees do happens alongside – and is integrated with – the work that is required. This final section looks at how learning can become a normal part of daily work.

Integrating learning into work

12

I first came across the idea of blended learning when I was producing eLearning materials in the early days of multimedia capability and the distribution of content for learning via the internet. Although a few over enthusiasts had heralded eLearning as the end of the classroom, it pretty soon became apparent, even to those most blinded by the hope and hype of technology, that a fancy computer program complete with end of module test was not going to be the only answer to the capability needs of the late 20th-century organization.

The original concept of blended learning was to combine one or more different modes of instruction to address the different needs of learners. For some, the need to demonstrate their knowledge of current legislation could be quite easily satisfied with an eLearning module, although the robustness of the end of module examination was questionable. Doubts were raised about whether the person apparently gaining credits was actually the same person who was sitting at the computer answering the questions, or whether they were really completing the quiz without looking the answers up. Further, the ability of the individual to successfully respond to the same questions some weeks or months hence, when providing advice to clients, or completing the final checks on a building, or prescribing a course of treatment, was somewhat unproven. The first 'blend' I was ever involved in was to create a separate means of assessment for the material covered in an online course by using simulations and actors to replicate the real world.

Thereafter, every client I worked with expected some kind of blended solution, even if a blend wasn't actually called for. The blends created settled into their own sort of pattern:

1 Pre-workshop eLearning module designed to 'level up' the knowledge of all course participants.

2 Pre-workshop quiz or test, with a pass mark of some description that the participants needed to achieve before being able to attend the workshop event.

3 Workshop event in which the content covered in the pre-workshop online modules was assumed to be understood by those attending.

So far, so formal. The blend was usually intended to reduce the amount of time spent in the workshop. This cost and time reduction was the return on investment rationale described to justify the costs of the eLearning development. Occasionally it was explained as being an attempt to match the required learning objectives to the mode of delivery (knowledge = eLearning; skills = workshop). Whichever justification offered, they all depended on a link between each of the three stages. Unfortunately, that link was infrequently maintained. More often than not, the trainer or subject matter expert running the workshop didn't know what was in the eLearning or didn't trust that the users had actually learned anything from it. To compensate, the content was repeated during the classroom session just to be on the safe side. What's more, organizations were rarely that interested in excluding from a workshop they had paid for those who had not passed the test.

One of the greatest sins in these technology dependent blends was that the end of eLearning module didn't test what people actually needed to know but merely their recollection of a random set of facts. The facts selected were the ones that were relatively easy to squeeze into four-option, multiple choice questions. The reason for the end of module quiz was that learning management systems (LMSs) were set up to work that way. Coming from a technologist's understanding of how learning happens, the original LMSs were fundamentally designed to support 'drill and kill' eLearning. These were linear modules in which user interaction was reduced to clicking next followed by a simplistic test. For each question within the quiz, option c and/or the longest answer was usually correct.

When discussing my exasperation at organizations' continued demand for end of module tests, my story was topped by the Kafka-esque eLearning experience recounted by a friend. At her workplace, the LMS selects people on the basis of an unknown logic to complete a regular fire safety eLearning module. The module is skipped through without neural pathways needing to be interfered with. At the end there is the obligatory series of multiple choice questions the correct answers to which are obvious to all but someone transported from the 13th century. Having completed it, each person gets to print out their own certificate. These are displayed ironically on the wall of their office.

After one such experience my friend turned to her colleagues and asked if any of them actually had learned anything from the fire safety module. Eventually one of them said: 'I didn't know what the different colour of fire extinguishers represented before and now I do.' The assembled group looked around the building. Yes, they now knew what a cream, black or silver fire extinguisher was for they agreed. But the only fire extinguishers throughout the entire building were red ones.

The system had effectively tested everyone's knowledge of something no one needed to know. The whole completion of the module took around 30 minutes, per person. It was completed annually. With 500 staff on an average wage in the UK that would equate to an annual cost of around £5,000 in staff time alone.

If you give the design of one of the most influential learning tools of the last 40 years to people whose educational expertise started and ended with the binary correct decisions of IT and mathematics, don't be surprised if their horizons are not particularly broad. Whether the understanding being checked was suitable for a series of programmed learning questions, that's what was on offer. Whether a pass or fail test to assess the user's ability to recall things they had seen only moments earlier was relevant, it was not at issue and rarely questioned. The test was the test; the LMS needs to record a pass or a fail against each registered learner.

The interest in blended learning, therefore, was in part because of the failure of eLearning to live up to expectation as well as the unrealistic nature of the expectations eLearning was meant to meet. But the extent of most blended learning was in designing a number of different kinds of formal training interventions. It was unusual for there to be much consideration for changing behaviour at work. The work-based application of skills and the use of knowledge covered in a course was not regularly a concern when designing a blended solution.

Blended learning comes of age

It's impossible to investigate 21st-century learning in organizations without encountering various models that talk about integrating learning with work. The phraseology may have changed over time but organizations have been seeking to ensure that learning happens as close as possible to the sharp end of what people actually need to do.

In most of the blends that were built, the use of the knowledge and skills in the workplace was expected to happen without significant input from the L&D team or the consultants they had hired to build online modules and deliver workshops. Unsurprisingly, the transfer of learning into real work activities was underwhelming.

When I first entered into the world of L&D the focus was on work-based projects and the mantra that 'the learning gained from doing the task is more important than the outcome of the task itself'. This was an important principle. The expectation that there would be failure and acceptance of that failure was integral to giving learners the confidence to dive in and try things out. These were not work in the accepted sense of the word. These were a simulacrum of the real world in order to provide learning experiences.

Unfortunately, not all learners could handle the setbacks of such experiences. For some, they lacked the maturity to stand back from the occasional car crash project and pick out the key learning that they may have gained. The ability to reflect and to be able to handle the fact that failure may equal a series of learning opportunities requires a degree of self-confidence and maturity that not everyone engaged in these projects possessed.

I remember well working with a group of difficult 17- and 18-year-olds in a vocational training programme. The group had been making a video as part of a series of learning activities designed to give opportunities for them to develop team working, problem-solving and communications skills. The resulting TV programme was good but not without its challenges – both technically and creatively.

In an end-of-project gathering, the resulting film was shown to other trainees who had been engaged in other projects. There were some elements in the final edit that were unintentionally amusing. Unsurprisingly, their peers laughed. Learning over.

In that example, the process mattered most to those organizing the learning environment, but the outcome mattered most to the young people involved. Not only that, the process of a public failure was simply too humiliating. There was no positive spin that could be put on the project and no route to rescuing the learning gained from the experience.

This individual project contrasted markedly with those learning activities that led directly to real work experiences. Work-based projects were about process not outcome. That subtle distinction meant that the groups involved had differing levels of engagement and motivation. Those who had overcome their initial reluctance to be seen to be trying too hard were coaxed and cajoled into taking risks. Those most concerned with losing face were occasionally helped in the background to achieve more than they would have done on their own in order to maintain fragile pride, enable some reflection on what had happened to take place and plans made about what could be different next time.

But there was a sense of unreality. This was not the same as 'doing the job' and however close the environment was to the one in which the skills would be practised in the future, it wasn't real. On occasions this kind of work-based project became a pretty good facsimile. When working with clinicians required to apologise for clinical errors, highly skilled actors made the whole process incredibly, and appropriately, uncomfortable for those involved. This was despite the fact that the clinicians were playing a role, the set up scenario was neither true nor necessarily related to the physicians' precise clinical discipline and the environment was not on a busy ward or in a packed outpatients' clinic but in a nondescript training room. However, this kind of simulation activity, whether undertaken in an hour as part of a training programme or experienced as a project in a real work environment over several days or even weeks, was not the same as work.

Where these learning projects did pay dividends was in the support offered, the availability of coaching feedback and mediation when things got heated. An independent source of expertise was able to assist in the framing of reflections. Questions based on observed reality could be posed to those involved that would lead to a deeper, more meaningful realization of what it means to 'modify behaviours, skills, values or preferences'.

The new blend

The projects outlined above were a kind of halfway house between the workplace and the formal course, with its presentations, exercises and group discussions. The focus was on bridging the gap between theory and practice.

It was also about creating situations in which learners could engage emotionally with the topic, think about how this would be in the real world and imagine using the skills in earnest.

Emotional engagement is important in terms of what we remember after the event. We know that when an experience touches us on a personal level and we have an emotional response to the situation, we are more likely to remember things. Memories that combine the factual with the emotional are longer lasting and less easily forgotten.[1]

Tapping into these more realistic situations is the role of learning designers and strategists who are interested in developing blended solutions to include a bridge between theory and practice and the integration of learning into the work. Clive Shepherd in his 2015 book *More than Blended Learning* takes an approach that goes further than the staged simulation exercise and reaches out into the day-to-day roles that learners must complete.

The basic process he outlines is called PIAF:

- **Preparation**: the assessment of the learning requirement of a group and the different media and methods that will be appropriate to achieve the desired outcomes.

- **Input**: the formal content component that may use any number of methods including, where justified, the classroom course.

- **Application**: the process of trying the skills out in as realistic a situation as possible. Shepherd includes simulations and role plays within this process where a supportive and controlled stepping stone is advisable. However, Shepherd acknowledges that these application activities may best take place, under-supervision, wherever the skills will be deployed.

- **Follow-Up**: this is the phase during which the embedding of the skills and knowledge into day-to-day activity takes place. Shepherd is clear that this is the longest stage. 'Throughout this phase, the learner is able to "pull" from available resources including coaches, experts, colleagues and content.'[2]

The shift from push – when the organization and its L&D team are determining the agenda, the activities and the available resources – to pull, when the learner takes control, is an important move towards informal learning. Where blended learning previously stopped, the process was still primarily push, however fancy the different inputs. For blended solutions to really benefit from informal learning, control needs to be given to the learner to take responsibility for determining their own learning needs and the routes that they will take to address them. While some learners will take a simulated experience and then extend their knowledge and develop their skills under their own steam, it can't be guaranteed. To really create the clear need for changed behaviour and the learning that underpins it, the learning needs to transfer into the workplace.

Moving to the workplace

Some staff development projects benefited from the realization that what happened in the workplace really mattered. Maybe, it was suggested, the majority of the learning happened not at the end of the content delivered by multi-media modules, PowerPoint presentations or classroom simulations, but when real people did real jobs, solved real problems and dealt with real situations. The work-based projects were just replaced with 'work'.

Except that the work needs to have been tweaked, slightly. Instead of returning to the same old, same old, employees involved in these new L&D projects are dealing viscerally with change. When they return to work they should be given new responsibilities and new tasks to complete. Their jobs should be redesigned to provide opportunities to practise the behaviours required. Coaching should be organized to provide checkpoints, encouragement and direction and to make sure that the investment in development is not lost through subsequent inaction.

The resources required to support those returning to the changed workplace have not always been available. In Chapter 3, I outlined the support for those involved in NG Bailey's Institute of Leadership and Management programme. These individuals who had been given recent responsibility as managers of people were also supported through external coaches and action learning sets with peers also undertaking the programme. In similar programmes, it is not uncommon for sponsoring managers to have specific roles to play and for programme facilitation teams to visit periodically to check progress, provide direction and maintain motivation.

However, these work-based learning activities remain an extension of formal programmes. The existence of the formal element – whether that is a talent management programme or a more traditional course – acts as a jump start to the process and unlocks the resources to support transfer of new skills and behaviours to the workplace.

70:20:10

Going one step further than any attempts to blend different types of formal training interventions is a model called 70:20:10. This model was first developed by Morgan McCall, Robert W Eichinger and Michael M Lombardo at the Center for Creative Leadership in North Carolina. As you may imagine from the title of the organization, McCall, Lombardo and Eichinger were primarily involved in leadership development and their model was based on their practice in helping people develop leadership skills.

What the 70:20:10 model says is that 10 per cent of the learning required will be undertaken via formal training inputs. These are the workshops, eLearning modules and even the simulation exercises discussed above. Twenty per cent of the time spent learning will be engaged in conversations. These may be with coaches who are specially trained to assist individuals to look at their own goals, assess the landscape and the challenges and opportunities they face and then plan action. The focus is on moving the learner towards the goals that they have set for themselves. This is exactly the same as the coaching activities we looked at in NG Bailey in Chapter 3.

Alternatively these conversations may be with peers, managers, role models or experts. So long as the learner is discussing their learning needs and planning how to adapt their current level of understanding to a new set of behaviours or a changed environment, these conversations are considered vital. These honest exchanges should support the individual in gaining insights about themselves, their strengths, weaknesses and areas where work is needed. It also helps to make a commitment to a third party, especially if that person is going to call you to account at some point in the future. It certainly assists to keep someone focused on actually doing something with the content they have been exposed to if there are a series of planned meetings at which progress, or lack of it, is to be discussed.

The 70 per cent is the on-the-job element. Lombardo and Eichinger were very clear that this component of the work is not simply doing the job.[3] They believe that the on-the-job learning takes place when individuals are undertaking 'stretching' tasks. These activities are situated in the workplace, but critically the learner will be involved in dealing with new challenges and new situations.

Most importantly, it is worth noting that the focus is not on some ad hoc process by which skills are somehow developed in an organic way through simply doing the job. Instead, 70:20:10 as imagined by its originators requires thorough planning and management of the informal, on-the-job learning if it is to work.

Over the last few years, 70:20:10 has been hailed as a brand new model of workplace learning and a riposte to all those who thought classroom courses were the important elements of training and development. Despite being seen as a novelty only a few years ago (although first published in 1996 and drawing a significant amount of its inspiration from Alan Tough's work in the 1970s) it has mushroomed into a fully-fledged L&D phenomenon over the last 5 years. However as with any new phenomenon it has also rapidly become a bandwagon. I was at a conference and exhibition in early 2015 and I saw no fewer than four exhibitors claiming that they provided the 70:20:10 platform. In each case, they made this boast because they facilitated interaction between learners using a tool based loosely on proprietary social media platforms and the opportunity to rate content and contributions with stars and likes. The 'social learning' component of 70:20:10 was variously described as the 20 per cent or the 70 per cent. The model had been enlisted in support of whatever these companies were selling, whether the claims were justified or not. As far as I could see, in each case the toolset being peddled was a learning management system with a few extra functions, but hardly an exposition of the 70:20:10 framework.

I have also seen 70:20:10 misrepresented in various ways outside the bandwagon jumping antics of a few learning technology vendors. These myths and misunderstandings include:

- 90 per cent of learning is undertaken on the job.
- This is how people naturally learn.
- 70:20:10 is based on significant research undertaken into how people learn at work.
- The numbers are sacrosanct.
- The numbers don't matter at all.
- The 20 per cent is most effectively facilitated by Twitter and LinkedIn.
- If most of the learning happens through coaching and on-the-job experiences why do we need training courses at all?

I actually think that 70:20:10 has some merit but I have seen no evidence that the model works at all if any of the three components are absent. The successful usages of a model resembling 70:20:10 that I have seen rely on:

1 Prior work experience that enables an individual to think about their current capabilities, alongside their goals and aspirations – 70:20:10 would be nonsensical for, for example, on-boarding or induction.

2 Opportunities to talk about these – occasionally with brutal honesty – with someone else. This person or people should be able to contribute knowledge of the individual and the environment in which they work to provide valuable insights.

3 Formal training that is negotiated between learner and tutor/trainer or coach/line manager. This may involve classroom courses or online modules. But it could also involve attending lectures, reading, participating in webinars, and job shadowing.

4 A chance to discuss the outcomes of these formal inputs, to see how they might be best put to use. These conversations may require a number of different inputs providing a broad perspective. They should also involve the individual's line manager where applicable.

5 A change of responsibilities at work. This could be a shift in responsibilities for a short time or for a trial period or a permanent move. These new, stretching tasks may be undertaken alongside and additional to the current job or could constitute a brand new set of responsibilities altogether.

6 Frequent check backs with coaches, sponsors, peers and experts; including…

7 Further formal training as required; and

8 Repeat the whole process until new skills have been mastered and work results match those of the top quartile performers in a similar role.

Does that equate to 70 per cent on-the-job activity? Who cares?

Does it mean that the amount of learning taking place via formal programmes is more or less than 10 per cent of the total? How would anyone be able to judge?

Is 70:20:10 just a learning management system with the rarely used facility to enable some peer-to-peer online collaboration? No, it most certainly isn't.

Is it formal or informal? Of course it's both and that should come as no surprise because it mirrors how people have developed their skills and innovated through work over millennia.

The informality within 70:20:10

The on-the-job components of the 70:20:10 framework rely on a degree of learner-driven informal learning. Done properly, the learner moves towards the top right quadrant of the informal/formal learning continuum contained in Chapter 2 and replicated at Figure 12.1.

FIGURE 12.1 The informal/formal learning continuum

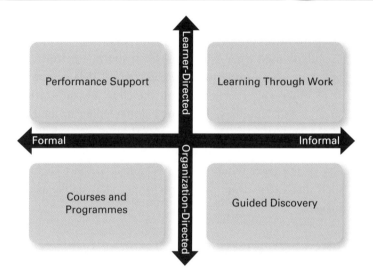

Stretch or challenge

In all of the informal, learner-directed development that I have encountered I have noticed that the amount of learning is accelerated when the learner has important problems to resolve.

As John Crossan said when I interviewed him about the work he and his team of coaches had undertaken with the new managers in NG Bailey: 'You don't want them to bite off too little and still be hungry.' On occasions, there may be benefits in relation to confidence building that derive from giving people simple tasks that are imperceptibly more difficult as each task is added. This is a slow process. It can make things easier to assume that a cohort of learners is each roughly at an equivalent level and have similar potential. However, this is a 'one size fits all' approach and if there is one thing that I am sure about it is that there is no single magic approach to enabling people to achieve their potential. The opportunities provided for stretching workplace activities need to be carefully tailored around the individual. Obviously this would be about the individual taking the lead in determining what he or she should do, but we do need to protect some people from an inflated sense of their own capability and we need to push some who would prefer to take less risky options.

Hungarian psychologist and management guru Mihály Csikszentmihályi (pronounced: Me – Lie Cheek-Sent-Me-Lie if you ever want to use this in a meeting) described the ideal balance between capability and challenge as 'Flow' (see Figure 12.2).[4]

Flow is regularly used when we discuss great sporting performances and there is something about understanding the concept that can be aided by applying it to observable excellence with the clear measures afforded by sporting success and ignominy. Imagine a golfer going around a course under par or a weightlifter achieving personal bests on each lift. In both cases there is a balance between the capability and resources available and the difficulty of the task. Where those two things are just slightly out of balance, such that extra effort by the performer can enable success, then flow is achieved.

FIGURE 12.2 Flow (after Csikszentmihályi)

The emphasis on resources is important, especially when we transfer this concept to the world of work. It is not only the skills of the individual that determines a successful outcome. On occasions a capable individual can be stymied by the lack of equipment, time, attention or an equally motivated and capable team or individual.

Challenge vs threat

In 2014 Ashridge Business School and the University of Reading published a piece of research based on observations of participants in The Leadership Experience (TLE) development programme.[5]

This programme seeks to prepare the business leaders of tomorrow. The start point for the TLE is an assessment of the skills and knowledge that business leaders have that they wish they had had earlier in their careers. Furthermore, the programme designers at Ashridge were mindful of the fact that most senior business leaders profess to have learned most of the skills and knowledge they rely on in their job through real experiences rather than via MBA programmes or specific leadership development opportunities.[6]

Initially motivated by proving their worth in a cynical business world, the Ashridge team wanted to investigate whether their highly evolved leadership simulation programmes were replicating the leadership learning experiences that today's bosses valued most. In order to investigate, the team undertook a series of personality profiling exercises with participants alongside learning questionnaires that sought to identify where participants were in four key areas: self as leader – a self-assessment of the individual's leadership skills; adapting to others; difficult situations and learning and development.

Over the course of the two-day simulation in which learners faced a number of critical incidents, conflicts and tricky strategic choices, the participants wore heart monitors. These were worn throughout the residential experience, even when sleeping. The heart monitors provided a proxy measure for the arousal of the participant's sympathetic nervous system. This is the body's response mechanism most commonly referred to as fight or flight.

The results were interesting to say the least. At points during the two-day programme, at the end of the course and some weeks later, learners were asked to rate how they were performing and how they were learning. What the researchers found was that when experiences, exercises and activities caused a raised heart rate the participants perceived that they had learned more and that these lessons were more long lasting.

As the authors found: 'In order to prepare leaders for the challenges of leadership, development needs to be hard-hitting, challenging, and present the potential for failure. Carefully taking leaders out of their comfort zone into the "stretch" zone raises their heart rate, and improves both their cognitive performance during the experience and their perceived learning from it.'[7]

The researchers also contended, although this was not the subject of the study, that in situations of threat, ie when the resources available were palpably not equal to the challenge presented, then enhanced levels of learning are not a likely outcome. 'There is a fine tightrope to walk between the "challenge" or "threat" response, and as such it is critical that these experiences occur in a safe and supportive environment.'[8]

I followed up with Dr Eve Poole, one of the report's authors, having seen her present these findings at an L&D industry event. I wanted to check that this was a step on the path to proving Csikszentmihályi right with his Flow concept and that a little stress may be a good thing. As Dr Poole told me, '… it seems that if you want both accelerated learning and muscle memory, you need stress to create the right brain conditions.'[9]

Flow has a deep relevance to learning through work. In that happy place of seemingly being pushed to the limit of one's abilities but still able to succeed, lays the optimum environment for learning. Doing something well while having to work hard and push yourself inevitably lodges in the brain as a benchmark for future activity, a standard to be bettered next time. That glow of earned success is also the optimum point for reflection and the ideal motivation for understanding what changes could be made in future that would deliver marginal gains in performance.

This positive emotional response to learning scenarios is also mirrored by work undertaken by Massachusetts Institute of Technology's (MIT) Media Lab. In their 2004 affective learning manifesto, the authors said: 'The use of the computer as a model, metaphor, and modelling tool has tended to privilege the "cognitive" over the "affective" by engendering theories in which thinking and learning are viewed as information processing and affect is ignored or marginalized.'[10] Affective learning, the MIT team argued, is about positive emotions. Although primarily undertaken with school children mastering mathematics, there are lessons here for the relationship between work and learning, especially if we wish learners to achieve flow at work in order to learn most efficiently.

We should also bear in mind the conclusions of the Ashridge research that triggering a threat response rather than a challenge response may not deliver results. In fact, the learning that may be gained could be to either:

a avoid those situations in the future; or

b that the individual lacks the skills to cope with those situations.

From a 70:20:10 perspective, we need skilled individuals engaging in those conversations that comprise the 20 per cent. These conversations need to go beyond simply checking up and urging further experimentation and risk taking. Sometimes the conversations we need to incorporate into on-the-job learning need to be protective of the individual. We must recognize that not everyone can navigate the fine line between enthusiastically taking up challenges and hurling themselves headlong towards stress and burnout.

Learning happens when the individual has been provided with the resources and the opportunities to learn from their successes coupled with the confidence and lack of excuses to be intolerant of their own failures.

Collaboration

The other issue with informality in 70:20:10 is the place for collaboration with others. As I have mentioned, this may be more formal coaching, leading the learning activity towards the bottom right quadrant of the informal continuum towards guided discovery. Collaboration may also be about peers learning from each other, asking for and receiving 360 degree feedback, and asking questions in forums or communities of practice. Crucially, and I believe more importantly than asking the questions, is answering those of others. The benefits of using tweet-ups, hangouts and other digital gatherings of the like-minded, comes less in asking questions and more in answering them.

The process of reflecting on one's own practice, perhaps undertaking some research to validate a gut feeling or reinforce an opinion, adds greatly to the learning from experience. Those who advocate 'working out loud' – commenting on and documenting one's working practice – have it slightly wrong. The benefits are gained from reflecting out loud. What's more an element of internal quality control should mean that those commenting do not simply express unsupported homilies and opinion laced commentary, but actively seek to back up their beliefs by reference to research. There's no point having an encyclopaedia of unimaginable scale at everyone's fingertips if we never delve into its digital pages.

Professional development

Despite continuing professional development and some informal approaches being taken to ensure that professional expertise and skills are maintained at an appropriate level, initial training for professionals is still seen as a challenge for informal learning approaches. Even Jay Cross, the standard bearer for informal learning for the past decade, when talking about the training of doctors, pilots and other professionals, admits that: 'Informal Learning is only part of the solution'.[11]

However, having established a base line knowledge and competence, lawyers, doctors, teachers, nurses and other professionals are constantly updating their skills and experience through informal means and through reflecting on their on-the-job experiences. Professor Michael Eraut conducted research into the use of informal learning by professionals in 2008. He started from a perspective of determining what competence actually looked like and boiled it down to: 'Where the practice meets the expectations of significant others in the workplace and/or among their clients.'[12] This it seems is an important point to make about gaining competence through informal learning. There is no generalized capability standard to be achieved. What is provided by experience is the ability to adapt performance to different situations and to rapidly weigh up the options and select an appropriate response within the specific work context. This, it would seem logical to conclude, can neither be developed exclusively through taught programmes, in which predicting every instance would be impossible, but neither can it be left to chance. The combination of a solid foundation of understanding and multiple opportunities to try out approaches, reflect on the outcome and draw generalizations and rules to govern future behaviour is central to learning through work and learning from experience.

Eraut notes that the achievement of a professional qualification is an important rite of passage and an achievement of a generic competence. This is perhaps nowhere more evident than when a medical student can finally adopt the title of doctor. However this is a rite of passage rather an end point. The junior doctor who has just left medical school (or, for that matter, the new teacher who has been awarded their teaching qualification, or the lawyer, pharmacist, dentist, or nurse) must now pass from the realm of being taught to the realm of experience and learning on the job. If we return to our informal learning model, the foundation of academic studies and examined knowledge is now the basis for observation, imitation and experience.

While the rite of passage may be less marked in roles outside the professions, there is no less a progression towards what Eraut refers to as **learning trajectories**.[13] These are the different areas of capability that an individual may need to work on such as judgement, working with others, decision making and what Eraut refers to as 'meta-cognition'. This is the ability to perform a task while continuously monitoring how things are going, whether the results expected are being achieved and whether new information has come to light that impacts a previous decision. Effectively, meta-cognition is learning how to learn from experience.

This meta-cognition is of particular significance when the informal learner subsequently needs to reflect on what happened in order to extract learning from the experience. As we saw in the Ashridge study a degree of stress heightens attention and enables the individual to meet challenges and complete novel tasks more effectively than they may have thought possible. Having a 'third-eye' may be of enormous value in the speed with which on-the-job learning builds capability and the degree to which learning through work is possible.

Multi-tasked learning

This would suggest that anything that potentially distracts attention away from the task not only reduces our performance but may also significantly diminish the ability to learn from the experience. Research with students at a Canadian university strongly suggests that present day, technology enabled multi-tasking interferes with factual recall. Students involved in the experiment were asked to both take notes using a laptop and use the device for other, typical activities such as checking social media, instant messaging or browsing the internet. The results were clear that students who were multi-tasking in this way were less successful in subsequent comprehension tests. Not only that, but students who were aware of the computer use of others – that is the flickering computer screens were in their eye line – were also less able to recall both simple facts and more complex material covered in the session.[14]

Those who are most enthusiastic about the use of social media as a boon to learning and as a route to enhancing learning through work often cite the opportunities provided by multi-tasking. It would appear that the level of concentration gained when dealing with an appropriate level of challenge in the workplace, and the meta-cognition required to gain maximum benefit from the workplace experience, may be significantly threatened by the tendency to attempt to multi-task.

CASE STUDY Learning through doing
in the Health Service

If learning informally through work is going to have credibility it really does need to work in pretty much any work situation. Medical training has followed a traditional professional path for a number of years – academic study combined with longer and longer periods of placement and on-the-job experience. As I outlined above, the qualification is a rite of passage not a certificate of competence.

In medical training, student doctors are now given experience of the real world of work in hospitals with sick patients as soon as possible within their first year at university. Amanda Hudson is head of education at the Bradford Teaching Hospitals NHS Trust and oversees training for some 350 post-qualification junior doctors at any one time alongside a significant number of student placements.

'The clinical placement was introduced in year 1 of a medical degree to address the relatively high dropout rates once newly qualified doctors were exposed to clinical practice,' Amanda told me. She explained that in the first year every medical student is involved in two blocks each of two weeks in a hospital setting to practise their communication skills and get used to the reality of a busy hospital. In subsequent years these placements will extend to three months in different hospitals and different clinical disciplines.

Beyond simply appreciating what life is like in a hospital, getting used to working in a team and being able to understand how symptoms may be presented, diagnoses made and treatments administered, the students are also making decisions about areas of specialism. They are preparing for the long, unsocial hours and the physical and mental demands and stresses of the job.

Through these on-the-job placements, students learn more about the nature of the profession they seek to enter and the hospital sets expectations and standards that the students will need to meet after graduation. There are also formal assessments of the placement through a process called OSCE (objective structured clinical examinations). These activities have the same weight as the regular written examinations. They also reflect the requirement to learn about patients and working in partnership with other professionals alongside knowledge about diseases, drugs and therapies.

The undergraduate experience may be work based but it still remains a formal process where the learner is effectively given learning activities to do and is assessed on how well they meet the standards expected. As Eraut outlined, the student's competence is not generalized but about meeting 'the expectations of significant others in the workplace'.

The rite of passage of the graduation ceremony leads the newly qualified doctor into another realm of training and learning. This time the transition is made to foundation year and a further two years as a junior doctor with lengthier placements and the start of decisions being made about further specialization. The junior doctors will undertake a series of rotations, designed to expose them to different departments and different healthcare requirements. During this time, new doctors will have access to a clinical supervisor and an educational supervisor. There will be mandated review meetings alongside more ad hoc support, where the newly qualified but inexperienced medic will 'pull' support from more experienced colleagues as they seek to become a rounded clinician.

Reflection is also mandated through the creation of a portfolio. Periodically, on-the-job experience is enhanced and added to through formal inputs, including simulations. Interesting, echoing the level of challenge outlined in the Ashridge TLE programme, the students will be involved in simulation sessions with trained actors, alongside real clinicians. The consultant in charge of the department in which the junior doctor is working may suggest treatments or investigations and the newly graduated rookie is expected to challenge and put forward alternatives. The verisimilitude of the simulation relies on manufactured mistakes to prepare the new staff for an environment where constant questioning provides a significant safety net.

'The objective is to bridge the practice gap,' explained Amanda. 'The learning is very much the responsibility of the individual, whether student or newly qualified doctor. But we can't afford to leave any of it to chance. Where there are significant informal learning activities, this self-managed learning is constantly monitored and checked. A doctor is some distance from fully competent by the time they enter the foundation year. But they all know that they have the opportunity to become a great clinician if they pull from us all the learning they can.'

Conclusion

Learning through work is the epitome of informal learning. If an individual can take a series of novel situations and challenges and mine them for formative experiences then the learning becomes truly embedded and high performance surely follows. What's more, learning is a habit. Recognizing that there are always new experiences around the corner, that things will change and that skills used in one context may need adapting to be relevant in another, is the sign not just of a learner but of a 21st-century employee.

However, we may need to help our people build towards learning from experience. We shouldn't expect everyone to be able to reflect on experiences and learn from them. Even if they can reflect on the experiences they have had, we shouldn't leave them to determine what is important and significant. Sometimes, an external viewpoint can open the learner's eyes to behaviours and practices that could be improved.

Organizations can model the behaviours required to effectively integrate learning into work. Through simulations and projects that are primarily designed to provide safe spaces to practise we can create the right level of challenge and support to enable our learners to develop towards being the performers we'd want them to become.

Some of the more formal processes such as portfolios of evidence, assessments and scheduled formal inputs may be required if the learning is to be integrated into work. Learning through experience requires some structure if it is to be optimized. The learner needs to achieve the standards for their own peace of mind. This provides the confidence to tackle different work contexts and ever more challenging situations.

The organization also needs some confidence and assuredness that what has been learned informally prepares an individual to fulfil the role required. It is the measurement of how informal learning has enhanced performance and delivered capability that is where we are headed next.

Notes

1 See LeDoux, J (2000) Emotion circuits in the brain, *Annual Review of Neuroscience*, 23, pp 155–84.

2 Shepherd, C (2015) More than blended learning, Onlignment, Chesterfield, p 63.

3 The 70:20:10 concept is described in detail in Lombardo, M and Eichinger, R (2010) *The Career Architect Development Planner*, 5th edn, Lominger, Minneapolis.

4 Csikszentmihályi, M (1998) *Finding Flow: The psychology of engagement with everyday life*, Basic Books, New York.

5 Riddel, P *et al* (2014) The neuroscience of leadership development: preparing through experience, Ashridge Business School.

6 Thomas, R and Cheese, P (2005) Leadership: experience is the best teacher, *Strategy & Leadership*, 33 (3), pp 24–29.

7 Riddel, P *et al* (2014), p 17.

8 Riddel, P *et al* (2014), p 17.

9 Email exchange with Dr Eve Poole, Ashridge Business School, May 2014.

10 Picard, R W *et al* (2004) Affective learning – a manifesto, *BT Technology Journal*, **22** (4) (October), pp 253–69.

11 Cross, J (nd) Controversy over informal learning, blog post, Jay Cross About Time, available at http://www.jaycross.com/wp/2012/04/controversy-over-informal-learning/ [accessed 2 June 2015].

12 Eraut, M (2008) How professionals learn through work, first draft of a working paper commissioned by SCEPTrE (Surrey Centre for Excellence in Professional Training and Education), 22 April 2008, University of Surrey. See also: Eraut, M (2004) Informal learning in the workplace, *Studies in Continuing Education*, **26** (2) (July).

13 Eraut (2008).

14 Sana, F *et al* (2013) Laptop multitasking hinders classroom learning for both users and nearby peers, *Computers and Education* **62**, (March), pp 24–31.

Measuring and evaluating

There is a phrase used often where I come from: 'You don't fatten a pig by weighing it.' Our obsession with measuring and evaluation can sometimes take us away from the real point of why we are doing whatever it is we are involved in. The short-term measures and the indicators of performance get in the way of actually achieving things.

In his 2014 book, *Complete Training Evaluation*, Richard Griffin argues that: 'The focus is as much on the learning organization as on organizational learning. The problem is that the practices used to evaluate the rapidly changing field of learning have not kept up with these changes.'[1]

Griffin has a point. My own experience of training evaluation is that it is over concerned with measuring inputs or participation levels and under concerned with measuring outcomes and performance improvements. One challenge here is that whenever an L&D team claims the credit for a particular performance improvement, the other departments from marketing and sales to production and finance will claim the self-same outcomes as the result of their brilliance. This indicates the level of silo thinking that we have in most organizations. The demands of our performance management systems means that we all have to shine and often the only way of shining is to make sure that other departments look dull by comparison.

In these intra-competitive environments trying to measure the impact of something as ephemeral as informal learning is not easy. In fact working out the metrics and the mechanisms can be more trouble than its worth. There is no point spending time and effort trying to measure something if the results will always be in dispute.

That is not to say that all measurement and evaluation is a distraction or unnecessary. I was once being interviewed about a project I had been involved in with the client for whom the programme had been built. 'How did you measure the return on investment?' came the question.

My client, originally from Russia and given to rather blunt responses from time to time, looked puzzled. 'Why would we need to?' she said. 'No one ever questioned the investment. Our company knows that training is necessary.'

For her, rather pragmatically, it was only worth measuring something if the resultant data was robust and rigorous. This meant it was only a useful investment of additional time and resources to work out if something was working if there was a feasible alternative to which it could be compared. My client had a research background. She understood generating and interpreting statistics very well. In the circumstances in which this programme had been rolled out there was no control group and so no data could be generated that proved that the programme of training and learning we had built led to improvements.

There are two things at work here:

1 The circumstances in which she was operating meant that any extra spend in measuring impact would have diverted resources away from doing what she believed in and – as no one was asking for the data – why bother?

2 The only information that was relevant was whether performance had improved as a direct result of the various interventions we created.

With informal learning there is a widespread belief that it happens without any input at all – which is true so long as you don't care what people learn and from whom. The demand for 'results' has been limited to those training and learning interventions that have a clear price tag. If informal learning requires no input, then where is the investment from which a company would anticipate a return?

This lack of motivation to measure has led to a lack of experience of measuring things that take place beyond the classroom and the eLearning module. The difficulty in measuring something that is informal has meant that there are few, if any, reliable models of measurement that isolate what was learned informally and accord a value to the contribution informal learning has made.

Now all learning happens in people's heads and apparently opening them up and seeing what's going on is ineffective and possibly criminal. We therefore have to measure the outward manifestations of what is going on in people's heads and what we measure instantly changes the landscape. Take the experience of LV= that I discussed in Chapter 5. They have performance data aplenty. They can monitor each individual customer service representative and they know how long he or she spends on each call, how often those customers call back and whether that CSR's customers would recommend the company to a friend or colleague. These are the so-called net promoter scores, a measure of satisfaction regularly used in retail and customer service settings.

At LV= they have recognized the potential dangers of communicating the average call time statistics to their CSRs. This is a planning metric, used only to ensure that they have the right number of staff to deal with demand. If average call time is used as a measure for CSR efficiency, the knock-on effect is that call quality goes down and customers don't achieve the outcome from the call they wanted. In other words, efficiency (call times) is the enemy of effectiveness (call outcomes).

What we measure matters. As soon as something has a number attached to it, the hard of thinking will revere the number and go after the 'hard targets'. It belies a significant lack of imagination. In a world of work in which 'people are our greatest asset' according to every glossy corporate annual report, not everything can be reduced to a simplistic set of numbers.

That said; there is an unhappy codicil to my client's confusion over why she should spend time measuring something when no one was questioning her budget. There was a change of leadership in the organization and an attendant restructuring of her department. She was made redundant and the role she previously occupied subsumed into several other roles with slightly different responsibilities. The programme she had managed for over five years had no high profile numbers attached and eventually having being unable to 'prove' its value was stripped of its resources in favour of alternatives that were new and shiny (though not necessarily more or as effective). After having invested over £2 million in this award-winning programme, it was quietly allowed to die.

Performance indicators

In the event that the preceding pages have encouraged you to think about managing informal learning – that is creating the platforms, tools, conditions and environments in which informal learning can happen – then you may want to think about how the impact of your work can be measured. Ideally these measurements won't create a significant burden on your resources.

In truth, if it matters it's already being measured. There isn't an organization anywhere that doesn't gather statistics that provide some kind of measure of effectiveness and efficiency. The measures may be smart measures aligned to the organizational mission – like the customer outcomes monitored by LV=. Alternatively the measures may be broader – for example organizational financial targets for profit and turnover. Where the broad measures are in place there will be performance indicators that provide some kind of evidence of progress towards the eventual target.

The fact that performance indicators are milestone measures or way-points on the route to achievement of a target or organizational mission often comes as a bit of a shock to those who have to achieve them or those who have set them. The word indicator isn't that tricky, one would have thought. Of course it ends up being shortened to a three letter acronym – KPI – and then it takes on a life of its own, quite divorced from its origins.

However ineptly these individual performance measures are administered, their existence means that the data is being gathered and the organization gathering the data wants these indicators of performance measures to be favourable. The most important measure of the impact of training and learning – whether formal or informal – is performance. Let's look at how we can use the data already being gathered on a range of performance metrics to provide impetus for our informal learning efforts and to justify these efforts to others (should this be required).

Example 1: the sales team

Every time I use an example involving sales, someone will complain that sales are easy to measure because it's about clear numbers. Similar to a league table in sports – if you win, you rise up the table, if you lose, you face relegation. Easy. The complainants would argue that most work doesn't have such clear target, numbers and indicators of success or failure enjoyed or endured by a sales team.

They are of course right, but allow me to illustrate the principle by using a concept called the sales funnel. If a sales team has a sales target of £100,000 per month and an average sale is £10,000, then it is fairly obvious that the team will need 10 sales per month. So far, so simple. Good sellers and good sales managers will work backwards from that end point and construct a sales funnel that shows the conversion rates as customers pass through the funnel.

As Figure 13.1 shows, the sales funnel or sales pipeline is divided into key stages. Suspects are the potential customers for the product who have not

FIGURE 13.1 An illustrative sales funnel or sales pipeline

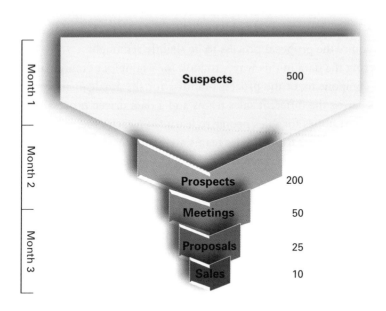

yet been contacted. Prospects are those who have been contacted and shown an interest. Meetings, proposals and sales are standard business to business (B2B) sales stages. In most B2B sales processes, there may be multiple meetings within the meeting/proposal stages. The time period on the left shows that this is typically a three-month sale cycle – that is, from the moment the customer is contacted through to contract takes around three months.

The figures on the right-hand side represent the conversion ratios. This shows that out of 500 potential customers contacted, only 200 will show any interest and only one out of four of those will be sufficiently interested to arrange a meeting. Half the meetings will result in a request for a proposal and these will be successful two times out of five.

A sales manager would be monitoring a sales team on a pretty constant basis to ensure that the right number of suspects are in the sales team's database, that they are making the required number of telephone calls to convert them in to prospects, that they have the right number of prospects at the appropriate stage of the funnel, etc.

The sales manager's focus is to ensure that monthly targets are achieved. She or he is interested in looking at the numbers from that perspective. The L&D focus on these figures is different. Are any of the various sales teams achieving higher numbers in any of these areas? Most importantly, are any of the team achieving higher conversion ratios at any of the key points of customer drop off? The most valuable work may be done where the numbers are smaller. Losing three out of five potential sales after a proposal may require a major change in terms of product or pricing, but it also might simply require the proposal process to be slightly rethought.

Analysing the data in this way – to look for examples of marginal excellence in components of the process – allows for the amalgamation of best practices across the different sales teams and a data driven process of identifying opportunities for sales people to learn from each other.

Does this happen? Rarely. Sales teams are regularly set up to be in competition with one another. Even when this is not explicitly stated, sales team of the year awards, incentives such as weekends away, restaurant vouchers or just having a mention in the company newsletter are all designed to promote a sense of internal competition. Short term, this may work but longer term it reduces and militates against the sharing of good practice.

The L&D team can be the troops on the ground interrogating the data and then investigating the reasons for the differences. Where this is about good practice they can prompt exchanges of knowledge, skills and practical behaviours. Of course, if teams that use these efforts to promote informal learning perform better than the average, this provides a justification for those efforts.

Example 2: the accident and emergency department of a hospital

If sales teams represent a pretty easy example of linking performance to learning activity, what about an alternative? In the National Health Service in the UK, hospitals with accident and emergency departments (A&E) are expected to see and treat every patient who walks through the door within four hours. Within that time, the patient should be bandaged up and discharged, politely told that there is nothing to worry about or admitted to hospital for further treatment on an in-patient basis. The target is for 95 per cent of patients to be seen within that timescale.

When a patient has not been treated within the four-hour time limit, a 'breach' occurs meaning that the incident is reported, investigated and recommendations made to resolve any problems. The frequency of breaches on a particular shift provides one set of data. The 'breach rates' or, when breaches don't occur, the average waiting times, are raw data. They are only meaningful when other factors are taken into account. Experienced clinicians will know that the range of patient problems changes during cold, winter weather. The average age of patients, the number of people reporting to A&E and any special considerations such as a multiple vehicle road traffic accident, for example, will all impact the figures.

The breach is also an indicator of performance, not a target. In the event of a patient coming into A&E following a cardiac arrest, not 'breaching' the four-hour target will be no comfort to the grieving relatives. If clinical need dictates that treatment is required more quickly, the four-hour target becomes a bureaucratic irrelevance.

Of course, clinicians know this, but there may be evidence of the four-hour target having an unhealthy impact on clinical decisions. If the review of the data finds that every patient was treated within the four hours, but that every patient waited longer than three hours, then it may be inferred that the department is being managed to achieve the standard rather than to meet the needs of patients.

By taking an overall, holistic view of what is going on in a particular shift, good practice can be identified and that proportion of reduced average waiting time for patients that can be ascribed to staff capability identified and shared. As with the sales teams, understanding the different components that comprise a simple headline target can help us investigate beneath the raw data and identify the marginal gains that each individual can learn from. Having identified what really makes a difference to performance, action taken to share good practice can also be assessed using the self-same data points. If performance improves for teams and individuals who use the resources created and the knowledge sharing that has been enabled, then it worked. If not, think again.

The performance director

In my 2013 book *Complete Training* I advocated the role of a performance director.[2] This individual in the business should be the board level executive with responsibility for the key strategic department. Usually, but not necessarily, this will be the function of the business that employs the most people. Their role would be to oversee the processes of identifying what constitutes excellent performance. They would provide the necessary authority for an internal cross functional team to investigate behind the raw performance data and the headline targets and work out what good looks like.

The changes to be implemented may be minor. If we describe the activity as 'reviewing the sales funnel' or 'assessing A&E performance' we potentially create a massive job to be done and weeks and months go by before a recommendation and a report appears. Consultants will be employed.

'From>To' PowerPoint slides will be designed. That is the kind of data analysis that will kill innovation within the process by holding out the promise of a brand new process.

This is not about re-engineering what happens but about identifying where marginal gains may be made by minor adjustments to behaviour, small changes in practice, slightly improved skills and a bit more knowledge. Marginal gains are the epitome of informal learning in action. They start with data.

What are you measuring and why?

Informal learning is primarily pulled by the learner, the learner is in control and manages the extent to which they learn. They control the changes they make and the capabilities they develop. Any attempt to measure the take up of informal learning through monitoring participation in informal learning opportunities, runs the risk of demonizing those staff who have not, apparently immersed themselves in our shiny toolkits and social networks. This would be a grave mistake.

The point of monitoring impact and effectiveness of the informal learning resources we provide is to improve the range, depth and quality of what we offer. Otherwise, we are in a similar positon to a shopkeeper who blames the customers for their lack of sales. It would be clearly nonsensical to do this. If the organization wishes to enhance informal learning it can't do so by mandating use, but by making the offers so attractive that everyone demands the access.

This takes work. Some of your evaluation activities should identify the extent to which the resources you assemble under the tag of informal learning are being used. The outcome of the evaluation will be to increase the attractiveness, and usefulness of any resources of managed informal learning activities. If your approach is designed to claim a link between your initiatives and the success of the organization, expect to draw scorn from your colleagues. If you say that something you have done has contributed X amount of revenue or Y amount of customer satisfaction you will be laughed out of whichever forum these things are discussed. By its very nature informal learning is not suited to being lauded as the driver of superior performance nor condemned as the reason for failure. The success or otherwise of informal learning is ultimately dependent on:

1 the motivation of employees;

2 the recruitment of people with enquiring minds and an urge to improve; and

3 the creation of a culture of continuous innovation and improvement.

Softer measures

Softer measures may be more important. Walk around your organization. Can you take a kind of health check of the business and its ability to sustain performance? The people and learning factors that you will review in this health check are pretty straightforward:

- Do people know where to go if they have a problem and are there any concerns about doing so? If this is seen as an admission of weakness or potentially embarrassing, people will spend useful resources that could be devoted to learning on covering up that they don't know something.

- Do people discuss work positively? This is about the buzz in the canteen, around the watercooler and in the car park. If the conversations are about how dreadful the conditions are, how useless the management or how impossible the targets are that they have been set, then there won't be much learning going on.

- If you ask someone what they are doing, are they able to describe what it is in a way that shows they understand it and which components of the task are important? This is about meta-cognition that Professor Michael Eraut believes is so important for professional informal learning (see last chapter). There are other indications of meta-cognition in action, such as alertness, focus, concentration. If you walk past a work area and no one notices you're there, that usually indicates a decent level of concentration on the task.

- Do people reflect on what they have done? And how do you know that they do? A good sign is if all the meeting spaces and public areas are taken up by colleagues in twos and threes talking about projects, programmes and progress. This is very often a dynamic opportunity for reflection. The meeting preparation will require a reflection on what has happened since they last gathered together. Further reflection on what worked, what didn't and what to do about it is the essence of these discussions.

- Do managers talk to their team members individually about work, skills, aspirations and ideas? I'm referring here to the regular, incidental, 'how are you getting on?' conversations that are the lifeblood of team health. Reserving these conversations for the annual performance appraisal or performance management process doesn't count.

- Do managers catch people doing things right? I have shamelessly borrowed this from Ken Blanchard's *One Minute Manager* series.[3] It was one of the first management books I was ever given and it had a significant impact on me as a very wet-behind-the-ears departmental head. The basic idea is that praise encourages more of the behaviours you would want to see than censure ever can. If people are praised for learning new stuff, guess what happens? They learn more.

- Do people who have been on formal training programmes have a proper action plan for how they can implement what they have learned and the further learning they may need to get there?[4] This is crucial and shouldn't be left to a vague comment that the course was helpful or good. Having invested development resources in an individual, the line manager and anyone else in the team involved in performance improvement should be ensuring that the organization is getting good value for money. It would be expected in any other area of expenditure.

These are only indicators that learning is happening informally, as part of the day-to-day endeavours of your colleagues. Their presence is no guarantee, but their absence should be a major warning bell. In order to develop some of these healthy learning behaviours you might need to encourage and reward their adoption.

Badges? We don't need your stinking badges

If you are of a certain age and humorous disposition you may recognize that line from Mel Brooks's *Blazing Saddles*. In fact it was itself borrowed from an earlier western with an almost cartoon Mexican bandit character. The use of badges and gamification has been introduced of late to motivate us to learn more. Colleges will use badges to encourage students to explore Moodle or other virtual learning platforms. Websites such as Trip Advisor encourage us to post reviews by giving us star reviewer status. We've already seen how the Curatr MOOC I used (Chapter 11) encouraged continued participation by using a leader board. In Chapter 9, I outlined how SAP entice people who are registered for free with the SAP Community Network to preview elements of the paid-for content housed in the learning rooms by awarding points that can be converted into training sessions.

I think these are good ideas. On the Curatr MOOC I took, for a while I became almost addicted to the leader board. However, I also noticed that some of the comments were about 'How do we get the points?' and the answer given was 'You just have to write anything'. What gets measured, gets done. Things that are rewarded take on an importance all of their own, simply by virtue of being the thing that is measured, scored or rewarded. I think we need to be extremely thoughtful to ensure that the behaviour we want is actually what is being rewarded by these attempts at gamification.

Borders College in the south of Scotland uses badges to encourage its students to log into and explore the resources available on its Moodle platform. Moodle is an open source learning and content management system and many schools and colleges use it as the repository for learning resources. It is also a vital source of information for students on the assignments they need to complete and the associated deadlines. It also houses Turnitin, a computer program to aid lecturers in detecting plagiarism.

The badges offered by Borders College come in three levels:

1 Bronze – Moodle explorer. This is for once the student has logged on, set up a profile and carried out the first basic tasks.

2 Silver – Moodle Adventurer. This rewards students who have accessed several resources, and

3 Gold – Moodle Conqueror. This rewards students who have demonstrated their ability to use most of the relevant functions of Moodle related to their course of study.

Now this seems very simple and straightforward and, given that the majority of the audience are 16- to 19-year-olds, it may be wholly appropriate. While the approach might not be entirely replicable for your organization, it is completely right for Borders College. They have found a cost-free way of motivating their specific user group to utilize a resource that will save the college money and time and make it significantly more likely that the students will achieve their qualifications. The key to its success is that it appropriately matches the desired outcomes to the awards.

As an alternative example, I once came across involved staff being given an iTunes voucher if they were top of the first month's league table for contributing posts to the company's new internal social media site. Two women set up an informal competition between themselves. It was to see if they could gain the top two spots on the comments table, **without posting anything of any use to anyone.** Of course, they achieved their goal. It is easy to post complete drivel on social media.

The key lesson is reward only the behaviours that you genuinely want to encourage and make the recognition appropriate to your audience and your organizational culture. With just about every LMS now offering gamification and badges, make sure they are right for your audience and the behaviours you wish to encourage. The badges at Borders College seem to work for 16- to 19-year-olds. They may also work to encourage people to write reviews on retailer sites.

We should be aware of trivializing through these rewards. By doing so we run the risk of trivializing the behaviour we seek to encourage. As well as the stories of badges motivating, there are also stories of college students not bothering to collect certificates, badges and even qualifications that they felt lacked currency in the world they inhabited. I'm yet to be convinced that the physicists working on the giant hadron collider at CERN require a set of badges to encourage them to share their insights.

What sort of technology platform do you need?

One of the outcomes of monitoring informal learning activity is to use that data to create the most appropriate platforms. This obviously assumes that a platform is required at all. There are broadly two sorts of technology platform that facilitates informal learning on a company intranet:

1 Transactional platforms: these are the kinds of Web 2.0 content management systems that act as a repository of useful information, curated content and 'how to' guides. I call these transactional platforms, because rather like commercial sites that offer product or destination reviews and user interactions, they are about solving an immediate need. This sort of interaction at work has much more in common with online shopping than with online social sites such as

Facebook. When designing most learner interaction platforms, I think the technology companies got it wrong. The social model was not the best option. Online shopping was.

2 Resolutional platforms: these are much more focused on collaboration. They are for sharing ideas to resolve common problems. These collaboration sites encourage communities of practice to continue the conversations they previously could only have had by phone or at expensive face-to-face events. What is more, they do so with a degree of transparency and openness that means that the discussion is open to others. For novices with an appropriate amount of prior learning, observing these interactions can be a step prior to imitation and experience.

The evaluation of what's really happening in your informal learning and the networks that support it can help you determine which the appropriate platform may be. LMS and LCMS vendors who are trying to cash in on an organization's desire to optimize their informal learning are tending toward the provision of collaboration platforms best suited to resolutional usage – that is the LMS or LCMS is packed with functionality that promotes collaboration without a clear purpose for that collaboration to happen. The problem is that it is likely that only a very small group of your workforce needs access to this kind of space. If the remainder of the site is utilized by new recruits asking basic questions, the specialists and thought leaders that your organization employs won't see it as being for them. They will continue to use the closed environment of email; telephone; Skype and invitation only web conferences. This will deny the organization access to the tacit knowledge that would otherwise be captured through a more appropriate platform.

On the flip side, providing a platform geared up to enable collaboration feels scary and alien to those who simply want to look up the answer to a question. The echoing digital spaces of the collaboration rooms will seem eerily empty and those who do use the site will assume it is unused and unloved. Forums in which no one comments are like playgrounds left in neighbourhoods where all the houses were demolished. They have a sadness all their own. I genuinely believe the presence of these empty, echoing forums undermines the attempts to engage individuals in using online tools to manage their own development. I only need to see one forum that extends to three comments from some months ago to know that this is not a resource I want to use. I don't come back and neither will your colleagues.

Artefacts of learning

Digital spaces do provide some opportunities to monitor the health of informal learning activities in an organization. These are dependent on the flavour of informal learning you have in place.

Think back to the General Pharmaceutical Council's CPD outlined in Chapter 3. You will recall how three out of the nine continuing professional development activities that working pharmacists have to undertake should start from a reflection. The individual is required to think about gaps in their current practice and define their personal learning needs. CPD related informal learning is a good indication of informal learning health. These days, most of it is managed online so once again there is data that can be interrogated.

If individuals governed by the need to earn CPD points are scrabbling around at the last moment to complete and submit their CPD forms, there's a good chance that these are not reflective of actual learning undertaken. Similarly, if all entries in the CPD are formal training such as course attendance, conferences or online modules, then what can be inferred about informal learning? I would suggest that there's a chance that any informal learning that is happening will be dealing with short-term issues and quick fixes. It won't be recognized as a learning activity and may be less effective as a result. Where learning is recognized as such, it usually means that reflection has been integrated into the process. Reflection makes learning stick. Without it we are simply providing answers and supporting the unreflective copying that Rahwan noted in his study (see Chapter 7). If the individuals were reflecting on what they need, setting themselves goals and taking responsibility for expanding their own capability, this would already have been recorded for the purposes of accumulating CPD points.

If you have a Web 2.0 platform where users can post comments, upload tools and write blogs, then there will be digital artefacts created. I would argue that you should be up-weighting those artefacts born of reflection – the ones that sit at the articulation end of our informal learning model. Blogs, intelligent contributions to debates, sharing of resources, tools and experiences – these all indicate that individuals are purposefully reflecting on what they have done. Whether the reflections are ever used by anyone else is not at issue. For the individual writing the blog or posting the PowerPoint slide deck on Sharepoint, the reflective process is that they thought it was helpful to them and may help others.

Performance appraisals, coaching conversations, team meeting discussions – these are all forums in which the amount of informal learning going on is acknowledged and discussed, even if it might not ever be referred to by name. Think about the average team meeting. The chances are that at some point, developments since the last meeting will be discussed. A good team leader may hand over to one of the team to relate a particular experience or success story. This is informal learning. The job of the organization is to capture such information and experience sharing in order to amplify it. Reflecting back to the organization that informal learning is going on is the heart of creating a culture in which informal learning becomes expected, welcomed and accommodated within daily routines. Most importantly it is regarded as completely normal.

Analysing performance

The most vocal of the fans of informal learning – by which I mean the ones who would happily consign all formal training to the refuse bin of history – are keen to point out that the only measure of learning that matters is performance. Of course, they are right. However, rather like my client who found herself made redundant and her major project decommissioned with indecent haste after her departure, I would advise caution against complacency. If we think good performance might equate to the organization accepting that informal learning is happening, is positive and is part of the mechanism that is delivering that good performance, we would be wise to think again.

I think we still need to make the case that learning matters and that continuous improvement only happens when learning happens with it. Of course, we don't need to continuously improve, we can simply watch as others overtake us and our jobs disappear. There is a long track record of organizations taking that route. As W Edward Demming once said: 'Learning is not compulsory, neither is survival.'[5]

The simple fact that informal learning is, in some respects, second nature means that our colleagues may overlook that it is happening at all. 'So what?' I hear people say. Well, that assumes that it will continue in all circumstances. We know some of this takes time. The freedom to try things out and occasionally failing, takes time and resources. The opportunity to innovate and learn from trial and error takes effort that could be devoted to the tried and tested. Reflecting on what worked and what didn't may require questions that some would prefer to remain unasked.

Most organizations measure only four things when they talk about performance and to some extent they are the only four things that matter:

- Quality – how well things are done. Whether minimum standards are being exceeded and what excellent actually means.

- Quantity – how much is produced with the available resources. Can more be produced with the same or fewer resources through working differently, employing new technology or via innovation?

- Cost – can money be saved or premiums charged?

- Time – how quickly things can be done – resource efficiency.

If you think about the measures that are employed across your organization or across your client's organization, these are the measures that really matter. To a certain extent, measuring anything else is unimportant; although milestones en route to success are valid. Without them success (or more often failure) can come as a surprise.

When things have worked well, there's a great deal to be learned from high performers. Most of us will 'get better with experience'. Consider this a shorthand way of expressing that we have been engaged in informal learning. Understanding what experience led to individuals who perform well getting better is a route to being able to distil what informal learning they are undertaking and to hold this up as a model for others who may choose to follow it. I would advocate a process of trying to capture the knowledge of high performers but also the ways in which they gained that knowledge and continue to hone their skills.

This works on two levels:

1 It puts the spotlight on the high performer and acts as recognition of achievement. Most motivational experts will concur that recognition of an individual's contribution is a vital part of the jigsaw of ensuring people perform well over a period of time.

2 It promotes the idea that experience is not some osmotic process by which hanging around for a long time makes someone better – it clearly doesn't. Instead, this suggests that high performers actually do something that makes them get better and stay better. The focus on improvement is important. As well as looking at high performers, the people who are top of the table, the teams that achieve significantly better than they have in the past are also worth identifying – their stories deserve to be told also.

Preparing the organization for change – the real requirement for measurement

Continuing to track these stories and share them with the organization is important because it increases the profile of learning and the need to continue to develop skills and learn from experiences. It is also required because change is constant. Organizations, like people, need to feel confident that they can meet change head on and adapt and work differently.

Of course, a disruptive innovation comes along occasionally and is either a rollercoaster we must ride or a challenge that requires more radical responses than the usual, incremental change we deal with daily. Disruption is an over-used term. It is also given an importance and significance that I'm not certain is always justified.

If you want to think about what is disruptive, think about playing solitaire. If you've ever played, either with real playing cards or on a computer, then you will know that the cards come up in the same order each time. That is, until one is used. That is disruptive. It changes the sequence of all the cards that turned face up during the next deal.

Sometimes what causes a disruption can be quite small and easily overlooked. The key to whether it is disruptive is the extent to which it changes the landscape. We need to understand the landscape of our organization to spot the disruptions.

An organization that knows it has learned quickly and effectively in the past will be equipped to learn again in the future. Without the stories of what learning is, when it happens and how it delivers benefits, the confidence of the organization to deal with change is severely limited. We owe it our colleagues to be story tellers for the changes they make.

Notes

1 Griffin, R (2014) *Complete Training Evaluation*, Kogan Page London, p 5.

2 Hoyle R (2013) *Complete Training: From recruitment to retirement*, Kogan Page, London.

3 Blanchard, K and Johnson, S (1982) *The One Minute Manager*, Fontana, Glasgow. For more information see www.kenblanchard.com.

4 In her book (2014) *Turning Learning Into Action*, Kogan Page, London, Emma Weber provides a detailed coaching led plan for how to transfer learning into the workplace after formal interventions.

5 W Edwards Deming (1900–93), was known as the US Quality Guru.

The informal learning action plan

14

In much the same way as those who always appear elegant in casual attire actually work extremely hard to look that way, planning in support of informal learning can be more difficult than planning the more traditional classroom interventions. As there is an art to looking effortlessly casual, there is an effort in being artfully informal.

This chapter contains four components:

Part 1 contains a series of questions you should ask before trying to develop an action plan for informal learning. As there are numerous forms of informal learning there are numerous ways of making it happen, or at least making it more likely to happen. We should always remember that informal learning happens whether we support it or not. Our focus is in ensuring that it happens in a way that supports our organization's goals and optimizes the value of people learning from each other. If you want to take on the role of performance director or you are working on your organization's strategy, this will be of most help.

Part 2 introduces you to the idea of the strategy on one page. It is an approach to action planning for performance improvement that was built out of comments I received after the publication of *Complete Training*. I have adapted it specifically for the purposes of promoting and enabling informal learning.

Part 3 is a kind of recipe sheet. If you read the introduction you'll know I like to bake bread. I also cook. Occasionally I will consult a recipe but I will rarely follow one to the letter. In the kitchen I am more akin to the jazz musician than the orchestra member. I see recipes as the basis for experimentation, improvisation and adaptation. I strongly urge you to view this recipe in the same way.

Part 4 is a checklist of dos and don'ts in pursuit of informal learning. If you wish to learn informally, or if you are the member of the L&D team given the job of encouraging people to learn informally without any additional resources, this is for you.

Part 1: the questions to ask

If you're new to the business of trying to manage something that is supposed to be informal, you may be wondering where you start on this journey.

The following questions (Table 14.1) seek to help you frame the journey so that it becomes manageable and has a direction and focus. Too many attempts to effect improved performance flounder on the sheer number of choices surrounding even the most simple task. Answering these questions should help you at least identify the starting point.

TABLE 14.1 Questions to ask

| Questions to ask | |
| Section 1: The current situation | |
Questions	**Comments**
How does informal learning currently happen in your organization or in the different teams in your organization?	It will be vital to acknowledge what is already going on. There will be some level of informal learning and it would be unwise to start as if there wasn't. People will feel ignored and under-valued if you don't notice the discretionary effort they already devote to ensuring they are maintaining and extending their skills.
	Looking at what happens in different teams and functions can be incredibly effective. Your future strategy could be as simple as identifying areas of good practice and replicating it elsewhere.

(Continued)

TABLE 14.1 Questions to ask *(Continued)*

Questions to ask	
Section 1: The current situation	
Questions	**Comments**
Are your people clear about their roles and the standards that they need to meet *now and in the future?*	Role clarity is one of the keys for organizational informal learning. If we acknowledge that we all learn as we do the job, then ensuring role clarity is the most important feature in enabling your colleagues to learn how to do their job in a manner that is aligned with corporate aims.
	If I think my job is to do something that differs from what the organization thinks I'm supposed to be doing then I am unlikely to direct my personal, informal learning in the right direction.
	The part of the question in italics is very important. When we talk about learning, what the job is now is of relatively short-term interest. Everyone needs to have clarity about what changes are on the horizon, and their impact on skills and behaviour. If your organization doesn't have a mechanism for sharing its vision with its employees then it will be much more difficult for them to flex their skillsets to meet the requirements of that future.
How are people currently inducted into a new role and a new organization?	Induction (or on-boarding) is a pretty important process in regards to informal learning. It will set the tone for the individual's future within the business. Ideally, each new starter will be given access to a buddy or a mentor within the team who will help them find their way around and find their feet.
	How does that work? What training does the buddy get in relation to the skills required? Are they promoting how things actually get done or how things *should* get done? Is there a difference and does it matter?
	The way induction happens creates expectations: the new employee's expectations about how they will be supported in future and the organization's expectations about how the employee will build the skills and knowledge to perform their role.

TABLE 14.1 Questions to ask *(Continued)*

Questions to ask Section 1: The current situation	
Questions	**Comments**
How are informal and workplace learning encouraged and supported by formal learning activities?	I am assuming that you have some formal learning activities in place. If so, then you may have activities that follow on from formal inputs, such as coaching sessions, mentoring, projects, assignments etc. Before suggesting new activities it is wise to assess how well these activities have been received in the past.
	For example: If coaching starts with enthusiasm after a course, but then gets dropped because of a lack of time or opportunity, then sorting out why that happens and taking steps to resolve these problems will be your first action. If line managers do not review training courses with their team members once they return to the workplace, then you probably have a culture that is not conducive to significant efforts to drive forward informal learning.
	If there are no workplace follow-up sessions from your existing formal training, this is probably your starting point.
Do you have any existing knowledge-sharing, collaboration or peer-to-peer communication platforms in use inside the organization? If so, what are they used for, by whom and how well do they meet users' needs?	You may already have some social tools within your LMS or you could have established a Yammer community or group on LinkedIn. You may support collaboration on your company intranet via Sharepoint, Alfresco, Google Cloud Connect, Samepage or some other collaboration tool.
	Check out how these tools are being used. Interview those who do use them and those who don't. Use this feedback to understand what value they add and how they could work better.

(Continued)

TABLE 14.1 Questions to ask *(Continued)*

Questions to ask Section 1: The current situation	
Questions	**Comments**
Can anyone post content using these tools or sites or are there restrictions that prevent staff from sharing their ideas or tools?	To create an internal resource repository of value, you need the capability for people to share information and digital artefacts. These may be documents, presentations, spreadsheets or blogs. It is not simply about authorship. If anyone can post something, how is that checked, tagged, indexed and promoted to people in the system? If we have a mechanism to capture new ideas and innovations, it seems a shame not to also have a mechanism to get them used by others.
To what extent do staff use the *internet* rather than the *intranet* to answer questions which they encounter during the day?	To get a handle on this, you'll need to ask people. Rather like keeping an exercise diary for those wishing to get fit, ask a representative selection of your colleagues just to note each time they look for an answer via the company intranet and each time they search via Google (or other internet search engine). Anyone can search via Google; finding information from the World Wide Web confers no competitive advantage for an organization. While using a search engine undoubtedly provides the widest range of responses, it will also include those answers that may not be accurate or in line with the organization's values and beliefs. The very scale of internet search results (I just googled 'informal learning' and got 3.76 million links) creates a cognitive overhead. It takes time to sort out the wheat from the chaff – time which, perhaps, could be spent more productively.

(Continued)

TABLE 14.1   Questions to ask *(Continued)*

Questions to ask Section 2: Problems, challenges and opportunities	
Questions	**Comments**
Where is your current area of dissatisfaction?	Don't worry, this is not an existential question. I am not your therapist. However, no one starts an investigation into informal learning practice in their organization without an idea that there is something that they think needs to change.
	It might be that you want to ensure you're supporting informal learning as well as possible. In this case the answers to Section 1 will have given you some ideas for future action based on transferring good practice around the organization. This is the best starting point and the most likely to be effective. After all, if it works in one bit of the business, the rest of the organization can hardly say 'it won't work here'. (Although that won't necessarily stop them trying.)
	If you have a greater level of dissatisfaction about informal learning or the transfer of learning from formal interventions to the workplace then you should be clear about what that dissatisfaction is. You may want to benchmark with other organizations to check out that your concerns are justified and that other organizations genuinely are doing this stuff so much better than you are. You may be surprised. A lot of what passes for commentary in the world of networked and informal learning is an evidence free zone.
What are the indicators that individuals in the organization are not optimizing opportunities to learn informally?	I'm not actually a big believer in 'if it ain't broke, don't fix it.' I think that the world changes too quickly for such complacency to be given credence. I think that we should always be looking to get better at things, to do things differently and do different things.
	That said, changes in support of informal learning are more likely to be successful if they are incremental. In things that require individuals to adapt, evolution may be better than revolution. Fixing individual indicators – such as having experienced staff trained as buddies in teams, making the intranet easier to search etc can be big jobs in their own right but may also deliver massive benefits for relatively little outlay.

(Continued)

TABLE 14.1 Questions to ask *(Continued)*

	Questions to ask Section 2: Problems, challenges and opportunities
Questions	**Comments**
	Of course, if the tanks of impending bankruptcy are pulling on to your lawn, I'll join with you in pulling down the statues. Sometimes radical action is the only sensible option. Vive la Revolution.
What would good look like?	This is the $64,000 question of course. Can you describe the sunlit uplands of a future in which informal learning works well in your organization? Specifically, what would people do to share their knowledge, access the knowledge of others, plan their learning and reflect on their experiences? This needs to be credible, of course. By using the data you have gathered from the questions you have asked so far you should be in a position to define a vision of the future. My personal feeling is that this is best achieved by a small group. That small group should not be an exclusively HR team. If this becomes a solution imposed by the L&D team, it will be extremely unlikely to have much impact. You should plan how to involve some people who represent those you would wish to have access to new and improved opportunities to learn informally. You need to elicit the views of their managers and their managers' managers as well.
Can you describe the benefits that would accrue from the vision you have just outlined?	Finally in this stage of outlining the challenges and opportunities, you should be able to articulate the benefits resulting from taking action. These should be at the level of organization, the team and the individual. The benefits that really matter will relate to: • Quality • Quantity • Cost • Time

(Continued)

TABLE 14.1 Questions to ask *(Continued)*

Questions	Questions to ask Section 3: Next steps Comments
Where is the low-hanging fruit?	You may find that your organization is sceptical about implementing a change to something which most people believe happens organically. Starting with relatively small changes and initiatives should provide you with a track record that opens the doors to the larger initiatives (with the larger budgets). However, don't forget that every initiative of this type has some resource implications. These might be as simple as a little of your time to monitor what happens, but it's best to have this understood at the start, rather than become a problem later.
Who should be involved and how will you get them on board?	This should be self-explanatory, but be clear about the nature of the involvement you are asking for. If you need your internal IT team to build you a platform, make sure you have considered the off-the-shelf alternatives or that that is the first part of the brief to them. One of the areas which is often overlooked is the engagement of the internal training team. They may have no specific role to play in the vision you have articulated. Regardless, they need to be involved in any case, because: a You will ideally want formal training and informal learning to neatly interlink; and b Trainers may feel threatened. It is not a ridiculous assumption to think that an increase in informal learning may naturally lead to a reduction in formal training. If so, will that reduce the numbers of trainers required?

(Continued)

TABLE 14.1 Questions to ask *(Continued)*

Questions	Questions to ask Section 3: Next steps Comments
	Having a group who feel they have something to lose and may be in a position to delay or sabotage your efforts is not an ideal start for any change programme. Best to get these issues out on the table as early as possible.
	This is also true – although the circumstances are slightly different – if you work with an external training provider. Informal learning requires a degree of openness and transparency if it is to work. Start in the spirit you intend to continue.

The questions above are designed in a sequence to take you through the change equation.[1] This is a useful process for thinking through how change will happen in your organization, regardless of the nature of that change.

The change equation

$$D \times V \times F > R$$

In this version of the change equation (sometimes known as the change formula):

D = Dissatisfaction with the status quo.

V = the Vision for how things will be once the change has been made.

F = the First steps on the route to change.

R = the Resistance to the change or the costs of implementation (organizationally and individually).

The important thing is that the formula works through multiplication. Of course, this means that if one of the values to the left of the equation is zero, then the total of the three factors multiplied together is also zero. You need a positive value in each of these three factors to be able to justify any cost or tackle any resistance to change which you may encounter.

Part 2: strategy on one page (SOOP)

Having answered a series of questions, and gained some support for your ideas, you may need to develop a strategy. These can be extraordinarily complex, but as no one ever reads them that would be a waste of everyone's time.

The strategy has two jobs: to communicate a clear direction and to act as a touchstone for more detailed plans and activities. In order for it to fulfil both its communications role and its role in underpinning action, you will need a structure.

That's where you might want to use the 6As as the basis for a good SOOP:

- Aim
- Activity
- Audience
- Assessment
- Actions
- Assistance

Aim is the overall goal – the outcome in relation to capability improvement via informal learning. This will require close contact with the teams who may benefit from sharpening up their informal learning practice. The aim will be derived from a shared assessment of the capability needed now and in the future for those teams to implement their strategic role in the organization.

Activity defines what you will do – and what you won't do – to achieve that goal. Will your focus be primarily on embedding subjects covered through formal training into the workplace? Will you concentrate your energies and your resources on encouraging information and knowledge sharing online? Will you concentrate on buddies for new starters or creating role models of good practice for novices to observe and imitate? Michael Porter of Harvard Business School said: 'The essence of strategy is deciding what not to do.' It's unwise to try and do everything all at once. Pick the approach that will deliver the most benefit for the least resources and concentrate relentlessly on that.

Audience describes the group expected to be engaged in additional informal learning activities. 'Everybody in the organization' is not a good description. Even if all staff at all levels and in all functions can access the resources, coaches or buddies, you'll benefit from defining some kind of effort on their part. 'For all employees who want to build a successful and rewarding career' is at least a statement that you expect a certain mind-set to be present before you will be willing to provide space and time for learning to happen.

Assessment – what will the result of the learning be? What impact measures would be expected? Remember that the only true measure of learning is performance improvement. If you are expecting to require additional resources to support this drive towards the informal, then it makes sense that you should be able to have an overall target for the benefits it will bring. This might not be an amount of money, per se. Staff retention, increased talent pool, reduced time to competence, etc are all valid measures that would:

a Demonstrate that you are serious about making a difference; and

b Quantify some of the benefits that will justify any investment required.

Starting with the end in mind shows everyone that you're serious about doing a good job and not afraid to have your work and its results transparently judged. This is about outcomes relevant to the capability of people in different functions. Credibility comes from clarity. Make your strategic target as simple and as easily measurable as possible. For example: 'Reducing staff turnover in the operations departments by X per cent by a specific date' is pretty clear.

Actions – this section describes the next or first steps. What will you do first? How will the rest of the organization recognize that this strategy is being implemented?

Assistance – describes the additional help you will need, including the role of line managers, IT teams or external consultants.

That's all there is to it. It's designed to be pretty simple and adaptable. The same approach can be used for formal training interventions. I think a SOOP works best when created in as much detail as can fit on one page for a specific project and within a defined time frame.

Part 3: the recipe

The recipe is designed to provide a list of all the things you might want to include in a project designed to promote informal learning within your organization. As I said in the Introduction, it is to be used as a basis for experimentation, improvisation and adaptation. I'd hate you to think there was only one way of doing this stuff.

Ingredients

You will need:

- A clear role for each person including an expectation that they will continue to learn and develop.
- A clear commitment from each people manager that their role involves supporting learning and development for their team members. This should include regular meetings with each individual exclusively to discuss learning and development.

- Standards of performance for each role – including entry level standards and stretch standards providing opportunities for people to grow within the role.

- An easily communicable picture of the current landscape for the organization and how this may change in the next three to five years. Regularly updated to ensure freshness.

- Trained buddies and experienced staff members who will be selected because of their high levels of skill and their track record of success *which they can explain to others.*

- A reflection process, widely adopted. A process based on What? So, what? and What next? is recommended.[2]

- Personal development plans or equivalent for each employee. No more than 50 per cent of the items on the PDP can relate to formal training.

- Elements of on-the-job application built into all formal training activities and followed up at an appropriate timescale after the training event or completion of an online module. If this can't be done, this information should empower you to delete that formal training programme.

- A technology platform that enables staff quickly to find internally approved answers to common questions.

- A technology platform that allows less common questions to be posted and answered within 24 hours.

- A site that enables staff members to post blogs about work related issues and provide links to resources and tools they have developed.

- Some bloggers for the above – hand-picked to get the ball rolling.

- A moderator/community manager for blogs and resources.

- A separate technology platform that supports collaboration in teams and across locations, including facilities to jointly work on project documents.

- All projects to have a project implementation review process that identifies key learning outcomes.

- An after-action review protocol that is used whenever there is an unexpected incident. Everyone should be briefed on what category of events would require an AAR and where the results of AAR should be stored.

- Curators (to taste). These should be responsible for cataloguing, tagging and indexing resources created internally whether by subjects specialists or generated by users. The curator(s) should also identify external resources that may be of use. They should ensure the most appropriate distribution and promotion of all available resources from whichever source. In some organizations, one or more curators will require significant subject specialism.

- Senior management commitment to learning. This should be evidenced by transparent executive team involvement in their own learning.

Method

Mix all the ingredients together. Communicate the availability of all these different resources, platforms and opportunities.

Observe carefully for stories of excellence and use the tools above to share the stories. Communicate some more.

Gather the statistics of usage and assess whether or not those who use more informal learning opportunities appear in the top quartile of organizational performers. If they do, communicate that as well. If they don't, change the mix of the above ingredients until they do.

Did I say, communicate? Well, do it again anyway.

Part 4: dos and don'ts

In this part I just want to list a few key behaviours (along with things to avoid) to gain most benefit from your informal learning opportunities. Although aimed at those required to learn, as this means everyone, there is no specific audience for this part of the action plan.

TABLE 14.2 Dos and don'ts

Dos	Don'ts
Constantly question. Why do we do things like this? What would happen if we did them differently? Is there a way we can do more things, more quickly, better and cheaper? etc	Accept the status quo.
Reflect on your own performance. What worked and why? What didn't work and why? Remember: What? So, what? What next?	Confuse doing things well with doing things well enough.
Find role models and work out why what they do works for them.	Believe everything you're told.
Remain open-minded. Remember that oysters need grit to make pearls.	Only gather with people just like you or with whom you agree.
Build networks.	Build a single network.
Write a blog to explain something so it's useful for someone else.	Write a blog so people will notice you and think you're cool.
Plan your learning.	Leave your learning to chance.
Give feedback to others.	Argue with the feedback you're given.
Recognize that results matter.	Think that the only thing that matters is the result.

I wish you well with your endeavours to learn informally and to increase your organization's ability to do likewise.

Notes

1 Originally formulated by David Gleicher in the 1960s and subsequently developed and popularized by Kathie Dannemiller (1929–2003), organizational development consultant and co-founder of Dannemiller Tyson Associates.

2 After Rolfe, G *et al* (2001) *Critical Reflection In Nursing and the Helping Professions: A user's guide*, Macmillan, London.

INDEX

Note: The index is filed in alphabetical, word-by-word order. Numbers within main headings are filed as spelt out in full and 'Mc' is filed as 'Mac'. Acronyms are filed as presented. Page locators in *italics* denote information contained within a Figure or Table.

Index

Index

Index

Index